FOOD LOVERS' SERIES

Food Lovers' Guide to Seattle

Best Local Specialties, Markets, Recipes, Restaurants & Events

First Edition

Keren Brown

Guilford, Connecticut

D0959477

Editor: Amy Lyons
Project Editor: Lynn Zelem
Layout Artist: Mary Ballachino
Text Design: Sheryl Kober
Illustrations: © Jill Butler with additional art by Carleen Moira Powell
Maps: Sue Murray © Morris Book Publishing, LLC

ISBN 978-0-7627-7017-5

Printed in the United States of America
10 9 8 7 6 5 4 3

All the information in this guidebook is subject to change. We recommend that you call ahead to obtain current information before traveling.

Contents

Central, 42

Capitol Hill, Central District, Eastlake, First Hill, Madison Park, Madison Valley, Madrona, Magnolia, Queen Anne, South Lake Union & Westlake

Downtown, 92

Belltown, Chinatown/International District, Downtown, Pike Place Market, Pioneer Square & Waterfront

South, 150

Beacon Hill, Columbia City, Georgetown, Rainier Beach, Seward Park & SoDo

About the Author

Fueled by insatiable curiosity to uncover every food-related spot and meet every foodie in Seattle, Keren Brown began by enrolling in cooking classes. She would spend mornings in class, afternoons scouring the shelves of the city's cookware shops and specialty grocers or judging food contests, evenings in restaurants, all the while chronicling her journey on her blog, FranticFoodie.com.

She created the Seattle Food Blogger Events—monthly meet-ups for local food bloggers—and launched a series of networking and educational events, known as Foodportunity, for the entire Seattle food community, bringing together writers, culinary industry professionals, restaurateurs, food companies and food-passionate people. In addition to her own blog she writes for SeattlePi.com and MyNorthwest.com. Keren Brown was named "Doer of the Week" by MarthaStewart.com and featured in the *Puget Sound Business Journal* and *Portland Business Journal*. Keren lives in Seattle's Queen Anne neighborhood with her husband and young son.

Dedication

To my husband, for his endless support throughout this book, tasting, sharing, and encouraging me in my food escapades. To my son, for being adventurous, making me laugh, and trying everything once. Thank you for being such a supportive family.

Acknowledgments

This book could not have been written without the unconditional support of the entire food community and friends ready to eat at a moment's notice. A special thank you goes to the unbelievably generous network of food lovers in this town.

Thank you to my editor Amy Lyons for always being there and for providing support throughout this journey.

I must thank my editorial assistant Tiffany Ran, who spent late nights helping in every way possible. Thank you to Kristin and Sara for helping with any tasks. Thank you goes to my mom and sister for helping with anything I needed, even if it meant reading about food that was hours away. A big thank you goes to all my friends, who were generously eating, sharing, and volunteering their help. Thank you Ronald, Michael, Candace, Jill, Alice, Chris, Andrea, Julien, Yashar, Deseree, Amy, Felice, Melody, Linda, Hadar, Allan, and Nurit. Thank you to all the chefs, shop owners, and bakers who shared recipes in this book: You have opened your hearts and kitchens and taken the time to spread your love of Seattle. Thank you to the countless amount of people who have taken the time to share their favorite dining spots, tips, and local establishments. Thank you to all my readers who have supported me throughout the years.

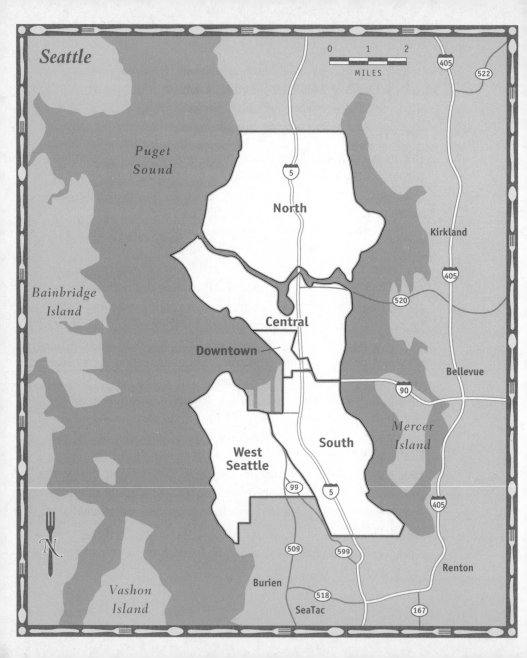

Introduction

Seattle, a city of 602,000 residents living in small and distinctive neighborhoods, is brought together by a great love of food, a shared interest that brings a small town feeling to a big city. New friendships, food inspirations, and business partnerships are established over the simple act of picking up produce at a local farmers' market. You might even run into a local chef or famed restaurateur, often known by locals on a first name basis. Running into these chefs on the street is as common as running into your next door neighbor. Those who dine out often will also be throwing in names of farms and producers in their daily lexicon.

Whether foraged or farmed, Seattleites are blessed with a backyard full of the Northwest's most diverse, unique produce and local seafood. Foragers delight in finding mushrooms in the forests, nettles by the creeks, and sea beans by the ocean. Fishmongers and farmers take pride in their ingredients, while artisan cheesemakers, butchers, chefs, chocolatiers, baristas, and roasters continue to push the boundaries of Seattle's playful palate.

For many, the Seattle food scene is a lifestyle, a way of life that embraces the homemade, the local, and the sustainable. Bakers using organic ingredients, restaurants making pasta by hand, and consumers demanding fresh and sustainable seafood have become standard. To pick up fresh bread, infused salts, and jars of fresh jams and connect with artisans, a food lover needs only to travel a short trip to a neighborhood farmers' market where questions are welcomed.

As for the weather, I'm convinced that we complain about the weather to keep this gem of a city all to ourselves. Yes, it rains here, and it is cold, but having lived in climates where the cold burns your eyes and where the heat takes your breath away, I've come to believe that the rain is a nice excuse for some takeout or a warm meal in a toasty restaurant.

SOMETIMES YOU WANT TO WALK WHILE YOU EAT. . . .

For those seeking a hands-on food tour, **Savor Seattle Food Tours** is your ticket to tasty eats and a cultural tour of downtown. Whether it's nibbling on Flagship Cheddar Cheese at Beecher's on their signature Pike Place Market Tour, or devouring Tom Douglas' famous coconut cream pie on their Chocolate Indulgence Tour, you will surely enjoy meeting the talented and passionate chefs and artisans that are the lifeline of Seattle. Tours operate daily and prices range from $39 to $69. Advance reservations are required. For more information and tickets, visit: www.SavorSeattleTours .com or call (888) 98- SAVOR (72867).

This is the ultimate guide to Seattle food. It is where you will find the local ice-cream shops, bakeries, and specialty stores. Here you will find the most-talked-about restaurants, hidden ethnic gems, and iconic establishments that made the food scene what it is today. And because Seattle is known for its wonderful ingredients, I have included recipes from local chefs and companies for you to re-create at home.

Let your mood guide you through this book. Whether you are seeking a casual night out with friends, a romantic candlelit dinner, or the ingredients for your own sushi night at home, you can find it among the nearly 400 listings in this book.

Explore unfamiliar neighborhoods, absorb new cultures, and pick up creative desserts for your next party. One thing remains consistent in all these places: You will find the passion that has helped food establishments remain successful in our struggling economy.

How to Use This Book

For the purpose of this book, I have divided the city into five chapters: North, Central, Downtown, South, and West Seattle. Since the center of Seattle is so densely populated with not-to-miss food finds, I have divided it into two chapters—Central and Downtown. Seattleites are familiar with the smaller neighborhoods that make up these regions, and each establishment in this book is labeled with the names of these neighborhoods or areas.

North includes:

Ballard, Fremont, Green Lake, Greenwood, Lake City, Maple Leaf, Phinney Ridge, Roosevelt, Sand Point, University District, and Wallingford

Central includes:

Capitol Hill, Central District, Eastlake, First Hill, Madison Park, Madison Valley, Madrona, Magnolia, Queen Anne, South Lake Union, and Westlake

Downtown includes:

Belltown, Chinatown/International District, Downtown, Pike Place Market, Pioneer Square, and Waterfront

South includes:

Beacon Hill, Columbia City, Georgetown, Rainier Beach, Seward Park, and SoDo

West Seattle includes:

All parts of West Seattle

Price Code

The restaurant price key applies to the price of an entree on the dinner menu; in many cases the price of lunch is significantly lower.

$	**inexpensive, most entrees under $10**
$$	**average, most entrees in the $10 to $20 price range**
$$$	**reasonable, most entrees in the $20 to $30 price range**
$$$$	**expensive; most entrees over $30**

Listings

Each chapter is made up of different sections: Made Here, Specialty Stores & Markets, Food Lovers' Faves, and Landmark Eateries. Each listing shows the name of the establishment, address, phone number, neighborhood or location, and website (when available). You may use the Appendix: Eateries by Cuisine as a guide to listings.

Made Here

This section spotlights local ice-cream shops, bakeries, chocolate makers, and artisan products. All of the companies have a storefront, and many are willing to ship their products across the country. Check their websites for information.

Specialty Stores & Markets

This section introduces you to the specialty shops, markets, ethnic groceries, cheese shops, and places to get the finest ingredients so you can assemble creative spreads for lunches, dinners, and picnics.

Dining Out: Tips to Know Before You Go

Restaurant Schedules and Menus: Many high-end restaurants are only open for dinner and closed on Monday or other days of the week. Summer and winter schedules may vary. Happy hours and brunch hours may change periodically. Some menus are seasonal, and some restaurants may change their menus daily. Check the websites before you leave the house.

Dress Code: Seattleites are known to dress casually. Most restaurants accept casual dress or business casual, except for a handful of higher-end places such as **Canlis** (see p. 87). When in doubt, just give the restaurants a call.

Dining Alone: Dining alone takes some getting used to, but once you give it a try, it becomes a great way to gather your thoughts and meet new people. Many Seattle restaurants have a bar area where you can feel comfortable ordering food and drinks solo.

Allergies and Gluten Intolerance: Restaurateurs have become more conscious of these subjects and are willing to accommodate. Take time to explain the extent of your sensitivity, and don't be afraid to ask questions.

Kid Friendly: In general, many restaurants are kid friendly. When contemplating the kid friendliness of restaurants, call and ask if high chairs are available, or ask if kids are allowed. I have found that coming in for dinner right when a restaurant opens is the best time for dining with the little ones.

Frugal Dining: If a tight budget is keeping you from dining at the places that you want to try, there are options to lighten the cost.

Many restaurants offer happy hours on food and drinks, so find out when those are. In many cases, lunch menus are less expensive than dinner menus, and during dinner hours, diners can order a selection of appetizers to share.

Seattle also has restaurant deals around town where you can dine at top restaurants for $30 and under during different months of the year. The 10-day promotion known as **Seattle Restaurant Week** takes place during April and October with over 100 participating restaurants (www.seattletimes.nwsource.com/seattlerestaurantweek), and the month-long **Dine Around Seattle** occurs every March and November and features over 30 restaurants (www.dinearoundseattle .org). Some of the restaurants participating in these promotions also offer diners a $15 lunch option.

This is where you turn when you need a special ingredient or a bit of motivation to cook.

Food Lovers' Faves

This is a comprehensive restaurant guide that spotlights a wide range of restaurants, from cutting-edge eateries to sophisticated dining rooms and family-owned ethnic spots. Here you will also find the newer, trendier eateries.

Landmark Eateries

Like moviegoers, food enthusiasts often seek out the new and happening, and the timeless classics may be overlooked. These are the tried-and-true favorites, iconic restaurants that have made it through tough economic times and withstood the biggest test in the restaurant business—the test of time. Here you will find restaurants with spectacular views and stories that define the Seattle experience.

Java Talk

Seattle is known for its buzzing coffee scene; it's the birthplace to popular coffee houses like Starbucks, Tully's Coffee, and Seattle's Best Coffee. But with new roasters and cafes popping up daily, one needs to spend every morning jonesin' the joe scene to sample it all. Here is a list of some of the cafes that roast locally, part of the ever-changing revolution of Seattle's coffee world.

Caffé D'arte (1625 2nd Ave., Seattle, WA 98101; 206-728-4468; Downtown; www.caffedarte.com) is downtown's traditional Italian roaster with its espresso blends, drip coffee, and organic lines. The flavor profiles echo a map of Italy, from the Firenze blend and its light qualities to the darker, more heavy-bodied blends of Taormina as you reach the south. Find smokier roasts with their traditional Balestra wood roaster that uses local alderwood.

Caffè Umbria, 320 Occidental Ave. South, Seattle, WA 98104; (206) 624-5847; Pioneer Square; www.caffeumbria.com. This wholesale and full-service coffee roaster focuses on Italian-style espresso blends and utilizes up to 15 varieties of beans originating from Central America, South America, and Africa. Here you will find blends such as the medium-dark roast known as Bizzarri Blend or the medium-roast 100 percent organic Terra Sana Blend. Stop by Caffè Umbria's flagship retail store and cafe in Pioneer Square, where they also have pastries, gelato, and Italian beer and wine.

Caffé Vita Coffee Roasting Co., 1005 E. Pike St., Seattle, WA 98122; (206) 709-4440; Capitol Hill; www.caffevita.com. (See website for additional locations). Since 1995 Caffé Vita has roasted in small batches on vintage equipment in the heart of Seattle's Capitol Hill. With multiple locations across the city, they pride themselves on sourcing beans directly from coffee farmers. Their time honored Caffé Del Sol espresso blend consists of Latin American, African, and Indonesian beans, and they developed a Theo Blend in collaboration with local chocolatier Theo Chocolate.

Fonté Coffee Roaster and Fonté Cafe and Wine Bar (1321 1st Ave., Seattle, WA 98101; 206-777-6193; Downtown; www .fontecoffee.com) is a well-known coffee roaster that ships beans within hours of roasting. With over 30 years of experience, master roaster Steve Smith hand selects beans and creates blends in a manner similar to that of fine winemakers, based on the varietal character unique to specific regions around the world. Their special selection coffees are comprised of the finest beans that reflect its special sourcing and distinctive flavor profiles. Try their signature offerings like the Sage Latte and the coffee Flight of Origin.

Fremont Coffee Company, 459 N. 36th St., Seattle, WA 98103; (206) 632-3633; Fremont; www.fremontcoffee.net. This old house converted into a coffee shop is one of the coziest places to work on your computer; its intermingling rooms and spacious patio make this the place to get a Seattle vibe on a pleasant day. Stay indoors on a rainy day and admire art submitted by local artists. Order a dessert made in-house and from scratch with your coffee. Roast master Aric Annear roasts single-origin, fair-traded and organic coffee that can be enjoyed in-house or at home. Whole-bean coffee can be purchased at their store or from their website.

Herkimer Coffee (7320 Greenwood Ave. North, Seattle, WA 98103; 206-784-0202; Greenwood; www.herkimercoffee.com) is Greenwood's neighborhood coffeehouse known for their straight shot of espresso. Their coffee beans are sourced through their direct relationships to farmers in places like South America, Central America, Africa, Indonesia, and India. Come steal a glance of their roasting process in the morning and enjoy an espresso, drip house blend, or one of the single-origin seasonal offerings.

Lighthouse Roasters, 400 N. 43rd St., Seattle, WA 98103; (206) 633-4444; Fremont; www.lighthouseroasters.com. Since 1993 this casual roaster has been a favorite Fremont neighborhood coffeehouse. Here the roaster is a centerpiece in the room. Try the Roaster's Choice, Mocha Java, or varietals like Yemen Mocca Sanani.

Seattle Coffee Works, 107 Pike St., Seattle, WA 98101; (206) 340-8867; Downtown; www.seattlecoffeeworks.com. Just a few blocks from the Pike Place Market is the 15-foot-tall drinking man sign that will lead you to this cafe with a designated tasting area. Visitors can compare and contrast coffees of different preparations and ask all their coffee questions. Call and inquire about the $6 tour that gives a behind-the-scenes look at the roasting process as well as the opportunity to drink and taste as much coffee as you want. Try the Obama Blend and Molly's Blend.

Stumptown Coffee Roasters (1115 12th Ave., Seattle, WA 98122; 206-323-1544; Capitol Hill; www.stumptowncoffee.com; see website for additional locations), were founded in Portland, Oregon, and are known for their true connection to the farms and farmers. Stumptown's green bean buyers travel most days of the year. Come in every day (except Saturday) at 3 p.m. for a free public cupping or to check out coffee roasting. Don't miss their selection of seasonal coffee or their popular Hair Bender blend featuring coffee from Latin America, east Africa, and Indonesia.

Victrola Coffee Roasters, 310 E. Pike St., Seattle, WA 98122; (206) 462-6259; Capitol Hill; www.victrolacoffee.com. (See website for additional locations.) The coffee is roasted in an old 1920s auto row building at the border of Downtown and Capitol Hill. They have blends and single-origin coffees like Streamline espresso, Ethiopia Yirga Cheffe Koke, and Brazil Pulp Natural Condado Red Bourbon. Eager coffee students and novices alike can get schooled in their cupping room, which features free tastings on Wednesday at 11 a.m.

Vivace Roasteria and Espresso Bar at Brix, 532 Broadway Ave. East, Seattle, WA 98102; (206) 860-2722; Capitol Hill; www.espressovivace.com. (See website for additional locations.) Espresso Vivace Roasteria, a partnership between David Schomer and Geneva Sullivan, focuses on northern Italian espresso. With years of research and tried-and-true techniques to developing the perfect roast, and a passion for achieving the perfect *crema*, Vivace excels in the realm of "latte art," or pouring steamed milk into espresso to create a design.

Zoka Coffee Roasters & Tea, 2200 N. 56th St., Seattle, WA 98103; (206) 545-4277; Green Lake; www.zokacoffee.com. (See website for additional locations.) The top-notch baristas here will enhance your coffee experience with a real knowledge and care about their beans. Zoka has blends, single-origin espresso, and

AIRPORT FOOD CAN BE HEALTHY

If you're looking for a healthy snack or meal while traveling to or from Seattle, then be sure to check out Chef Kathy Casey's **Dish D'Lish**® (Seattle-Tacoma International Airport; www.dishdlish .com; $). Whether eating-in or grabbing Food T' Go Go®, there are plenty of market-fresh foods and beverages to choose from— made daily on-site. Tasty examples include a hand-shaken NW berry lemonade; savory stratas made with rustic bread, eggs, cheese and savory goodies baked 'til golden—great for breakfast, lunch, or a quick snack; The NW Salad featuring house greens, roasted pears, toasted hazelnuts, blue cheese and cranberry vinaigrette; and Kathy's favorite hot pressed sandwich made with house roasted chicken, brie, and Washington apple chutney. Travelers can also pick up Kathy's latest cookbooks and specialty products. See Chef Kathy Casey's recipe for **Citrus 75** on p. 188.

other coffee beverages. Espresso Paladino is their crowd pleaser, made of 100 percent arabica coffees of South American, Indonesian, and African origin.

Trucks or Bust

Over the past couple of years or so, roaming restaurants in the form of food trucks have been satisfying the Seattleite's need for quick and diverse lunches. Facebook pages, websites, and Twitter updates make it easy for avid diners to track their locations down for a quick lunch, dinner, or mid-afternoon snack. To get a taste of many trucks in one place, follow the mobile chowdown website for their food trucks events http://themobilechowdown.com.

Skillet Street Food (www.skilletstreetfood.com; Twitter: @skilletstfood) is where you get American comfort food out of an airstream trailer. Here the burgers are topped with their famous bacon jam that can also be ordered online. Don't forget the *poutine*—fries, gravy, and melted cheese. For Mexican food, find **El Camion** (www.elcamion seattle.com; Twitter: @elcamionseattle). For a mix of Korean and Hawaiian fusion, head toward the **Marination Mobile** (www.marinationmobile.com; Twitter: @curbcuisine), with items like miso ginger chicken and kimchee rice bowls. For bursting pitas full of falafel or *shawarma*, check out the yellow

truck in Georgetown known as **Hallava Falafel** (http://hallavafalafel
.com; see p. 161 for more information). Look for po'boys, Muffulettas,
and beignets at **Where Ya at Matt,** a truck with cuisine from New Orleans
(www.whereyaatmatt.com; Twitter: @WhereYaAtMatt). If you see a
pig on wheels, it must be **Maximus/Minimus** (www.maximus-minimus
.com; Twitter: @somepigseattle) serving pulled pork and vegetarian
sandwiches either spicy (Maximus) or sweet (Minimus). Find the Thai-
Hawaiian-style plate lunches at **Pai's** (www.paifoods.com; Twitter: @
paifoods), or for items like pad thai or red curry, visit the Thai food
truck by the name of **Kaosamai** (www.kaosamai.com; Twitter: @thai
foodtruck; or stop by their restaurant at 404 N. 36th St., Seattle, WA
98103; 206-925-9979; Fremont). Let your sweet tooth guide you with
Sweet Treats (www.streettreatswa.com; Twitter: @StreetTreatsWA),
and for a cold treat, try the modern day ice-cream trucks from **Molly
Moon's Homemade Ice Cream** (www.mollymoonicecream.com; Twitter:
@mollymoon; see more in North chapter), or **Parfait Ice Cream** (www
.parfaiticecream.com; Twitter: @ParfaitIceCream). For that hot dog
craving, look no further then **Dante's Inferno Dogs** (www.dantes
infernodogs.com; Twitter: @Danteinfernodog).

Vegetarian Dining

Chefs here love fresh produce, and vegetarian options can be found
on almost every menu. If you are looking for a fancy night out,
opt for the course-by-course tasting menus presented at **Canlis**

(see p. 87), **Tilth** (see p. 35), or **Rover's** (see p. 90). **Poppy**'s (see p. 79) vegetarian *thali* is sure to surprise with playful vegetable combinations. Landmark restaurants like **Cafe Flora** (see p. 86) or **Carmelita** (see p. 39) have rightfully earned their loyal followings. **Sutra** (1605 N. 45th St., Seattle, WA 98103; 206-547-1348; www.sutraseattle.com) is a dining experience akin to a private supper club with a four-course pre-fixe menu. Capitol Hill's vegan restaurant by the name of **Plum Bistro** (1429 12th Ave., Seattle, WA 98122; 206-838-5333) is a fabulous choice for a light bites, lunch, brunch, or dinner. An extensive vegetarian menu can be found at **Chaco Canyon Organic Cafe** (4757 12th Ave. Northeast, Seattle, WA 98105; 206-522-6966; www.chacocanyoncafe.com) as well as vegan sandwiches, rice bowls, breakfast items, and raw entrees. For the raw curious, experience **Thrive** (1026 N.E. 65th St., #A102, Seattle, WA 98115; 206-525-0300; www.generation thrive.com) with delicious sauces and imaginative takes on items like teriyaki, salads, and desserts. For Thai food, stop by **Araya's Vegetarian Place** (1121 N.E. 45th St., Seattle, WA 98105; 206-524-4332; http://arayasplace.com; University District) or **Jhanjay** (1718 N. 45th St., Seattle, WA 98103; 206-626-1484; Wallingford; second location at 5313B Ballard Ave. NW, Seattle, WA 98107; 206-588-1469; www.jhanjay.com), and for the adventurous, go for the spicy Ethiopian at **Meskel** (see p. 76).

North

In the north part of Seattle, Ballard was once the home of Scandinavian fishermen. Today it's a young, artsy neighborhood, a destination for diners avoiding downtown congestion, thriving with its art walk, restaurants, and bar scene. Ballard now boasts an oyster bar, a waterfront restaurant in the form of a boathouse, trendy taverns with live music, and some Northwest-inspired restaurants. The University District, aka the "U District," is a thriving area packed with students from the University of Washington. Known as "the Ave," University Way Northeast is a series of blocks with a melting pot of modestly priced dining options and pastry-laden coffeehouses. University Village is a large open-air shopping center with well-dressed customers and high-quality boutiques as well as a cupcake shop, a chocolate shop, and an old-fashioned candy shop. Healthy eaters, hippies, and laid-back types will love the Fremont neighborhood with its fashionable shops, healthy stores, outdoor market, and chocolate factory that you can smell from afar.

In this chapter you will find the neighborhoods Ballard, Fremont, Green Lake, Greenwood, Lake City, Maple Leaf, Phinney Ridge, Roosevelt, Sand Point, University District, and Wallingford.

60th Street Desserts, 7401 Sand Point Way Northeast, Seattle, WA 98115; (206) 527-8560; Sand Point; www.60thstreetdesserts .com. For those mornings when you wake up on the wrong side of the bed, this drive-through window is your savior. Start your morning with any of these menu items: scones, breakfast burritos, brownies, custard bars, coffee cakes, homemade soups, sandwiches made with their freshly baked oat breads or focaccia, and more. Joan Williams opened this bakery on 60th Street in 1988 as a wholesale bakery because she wanted to find something she could do while spending time with her two daughters. Though the location later moved to Sand Point Way, Joan knew that retail was her calling. It started with her passing desserts to her fans through a Dutch door and evolved into a drive-through business. Busy parents can drive by and pick up baked appetizers, entrees, desserts, and pizza dough. The best seller here is the marionberry cheesecake.

Bottega Italiana, 409 N.E. 70th St., Seattle, WA 98115; (206) 524-4416; Green Lake; www.bottegaitaliana.com. For a full description see the Downtown listing, p. 94.

Cafe Besalu, 5909 24th Ave. Northwest, Seattle, WA 98107; (206) 789-1463; Ballard; www.cafebesalu.com. Walking into this little French cafe is like walking into a buttery heaven. Surrender to the aroma while you decide which pastry will launch your day. Peek over the sides of the glass to watch dough being rolled out in front of your eyes. The tarts are made with fresh fruit, and there are uniquely light and fluffy ginger biscuits, buttery croissants, and a killer *pain au chocolat*. This is *the* place you'd want to be reading your morning paper.

Cupcake Royale and Vérité Coffee, 1101 34th Ave., Seattle, WA 98122; (206) 709-4497; Madrona; www.cupcakeroyale.com. For a full description see the Central listing, p. 44.

The Dahlia Workshop, 401 Westlake Ave. North, Seattle, WA 98122; (206) 436-0052; South Lake Union. Right downstairs from Serious Pie Westlake and Harrison, lies Tom Douglas' quaint little biscuit shop that is open daily until 2 p.m. Get some fresh-out-of-the-oven buttermilk biscuits with options like fried chicken with Tabasco, black pepper gravy, and a fried egg; or "the workshop" featuring house-cured ham, cheddar, and apple mustard and a fried egg; or fried green tomato, bacon, and remoulade with, you guessed it, a fried egg. Salads and soups are available as sides. The small seating area makes this an ideal place for breakfast or lunch on the go. After 5 p.m. every day the space is transformed into a wine bar serving hand-chipped prosciutto di parma.

D'Ambrosio Gelato, 5339 Ballard Ave. Northwest, Seattle, WA 98107; (206) 327-9175; Ballard; www.dambrosiogelato.com.

Italian-born Marco D'Ambrosio had been working in the wine industry in Seattle for five and a half years when he convinced his dad, Enzo, a university-certified gelato master, to open this gelato shop in the heart of Ballard. Many of the ingredients, such as the hazelnuts, white chocolate, and jams are imported from Italy, giving the gelato a *unico* intensity. The dairy and fruit come from local organic sources when possible. The most popular flavor is the *pistacchio di bronte* made with an imported Sicilian pistachio produced in Bronte, Italy, near the Etna volcano, known for its intense and aromatic flavor. Other interesting flavors are the lemon; coconut hazelnut; and the *Fichi, Mascarpone & Caramello*, a mix of mascarpone, figs, and caramel. A small cone starts at $3.50 and includes 2 flavors. Don't let the line out the door dissuade you of this Italian luxury; it seems to move pretty fast.

The Erotic Bakery, 2323 N. 45th St., Seattle, WA 98103; (206) 545-6969; Wallingford; www.theeroticbakery.com. The rapport between food and sexuality has been around forever. Mother Nature is responsible for driving us bananas with a bounty of fruits whose very shapes are similar to the human body. The Erotic Bakery pushes the boundaries by melding food and sexuality with their humorous and tasty cakes. Disclaimer: Enter at your own risk and leave your inhibitions at home. Erotic has phallic-shaped cakes with all the trimmings, cookies with marzipan bosoms, cheesecakes designed with naughty body parts, and assorted party platters in all shapes and sizes. Have an uncommon request for a cake? Don't fret. They custom-design many cakes for bachelor and bachelorette parties or events; no request is too racy. Cakes can be ordered online. The cakes may be a little pricey, but the looks on the faces of your friends? Priceless.

The Essential Baking Company, 1604 N. 34th St., Seattle, WA 98103; (206) 545-0444; Wallingford; www.essentialbaking .com. (See website for additional locations.) Seattle's first local, certified-organic, artisanal bakery, the Essential Baking Company, was founded in 1994. Using organic and natural ingredients and no preservatives, Essential makes fresh handcrafted artisan breads, European pastries, and luscious desserts. All locations boast a generous seating area, knowledgeable staff, and a wide selection of breads, quiches, scones, bars, muffins, and more. Order a loaf of the rosemary diamante, made of fresh organic rosemary, durum flour, and sprinkled with sea salt; a cinnamon roll; or the Chocolate Indulgence cookie. See Essential Baking Company's recipe for **Vegetarian Strata** on p. 201.

Fainting Goat Gelato, 1903 N. 45th St., Seattle, WA 98103; (206) 327-9459; Wallingford; www.faintinggoatseattle.com. This is the story of a Turkish family who moves to Seattle and decides to open a gelato shop. Why gelato? They found gelato to be similar to the Turkish ice cream that they had grown to love. They use local organic dairy from Lynden, Washington's **Fresh Breeze Organic Dairy** as well as organic sugar and other ingredients. The most popular flavors include salted caramel, pistachio, and hazelnut. The most original flavor is the goat milk gelato made with mastic gum, a tree resin that possesses a piney vanilla flavor. The space is family friendly with a table for the kiddos and Turkish coffee to keep the big kids happy.

Fran's Chocolates, 2626 N.E. University Village St., Seattle, WA 98105; (206) 528-9969; University District; www.franschocolates .com. (See website for additional locations.) Fran Bigelow started Fran's Chocolates over 28 years ago after falling in love with the chocolate culture in Paris. A pioneer in the Seattle chocolate industry, Fran produces chocolate in small batches using all-natural and organic ingredients (when possible) and the finest cacao from Venezuela, Madagascar, and Ecuador. Even the Obamas have professed their love for this Seattle favorite; the president favors Fran's Smoked Sea Salt Caramel in Milk Chocolate. Fran's has been mentioned by *Martha Stewart Living, O Magazine,* and other national publications. If that isn't recognition enough, *Jeopardy* featured Fran's Grey Salt Caramels in an $800 question in 2008. Go for the Grey Salt Caramels, Smoked Salt Caramels, and the Almond Gold Bars.

Fresh Flours, 6015 Phinney Ave. North, Seattle, WA 98103; (206) 297-3300; Phinney Ridge; and 5313 Ballard Ave. Northwest, Seattle WA 98107; (206) 706-3338; Ballard; www.freshfloursseattle

.com. With two locations, Fresh Flours is a neighborhood bakery that showcases fresh sweets with a Japanese twist. In addition to classic bakery items like raspberry and blueberry muffins and croissants, you will find interesting items like lemon-ginger muffins, green-tea muffins, green-tea *macarons,* and adzuki-bean cream brioche. They also have sandwiches, quiches, Stumptown Coffee, and a cozy seating area. See Fresh Flours' recipe for **Green Tea Checkerboard Cookies** on p. 207.

Full Tilt, 4759 Brooklyn Ave. Northeast, Seattle, WA 98105; (206) 524-4406; University District; www.fulltilticecream.com. This mini location of Full Tilt has the same creative ice-cream flavors but only one video game. (Check the Columbia City listing, p. 152, for the full deal.)

Hiroki, 2224 N. 56th St., Seattle, WA 98103; (206) 547-4128; Green Lake; www.hiroki.us. Nothing beats catching up with an old friend over a slice of cake. Chef Hiroki's bakery-cafe is the perfect place for friendly conversation and bonding over his Japanese/European-style desserts. You will find baked items like perfectly crafted éclairs, cream puffs, Chocolate Chocolate Orange Cookies, and Peach Custard Bread. I recommend the Green Tea Tiramisu. Closed Mon and Tues.

Honore Artisan Bakery, 1413 N.W. 70th St., Seattle, WA 98117; (206) 706-4035; Ballard. Hidden in a quaint residential area of Ballard lies a petite bakery with rainbows of French *macarons.*

Imagine symmetrical circles, sandwiched with cream and infused with a burst of flavor. Varieties include lavender, pistachio, coffee, chocolate, and coconut–salted caramel, just to name a few. When you're done choosing the colorful macarons to take home, choose a croissant, the quiche, or the *kouign amann,* a Breton cake, made with butter and sea salt, a splendid marriage of savory and sweet. On summer days, the patio out back is a nice surprise. This is the perfect place to pick up pastries when guests are coming over, but take note, the place has limited seating and hours. Open Wed through Fri 7 a.m. to 4 p.m., and weekends 8 a.m. to 4 p.m.

Larsen's Danish Bakery, 8000 24th Ave. Northwest, Seattle, WA 98117; (800) 626-8631; Ballard; www.larsensbakery.com. It seems like people either love or hate marzipan. If you are part of the marzipan fan club, I suggest that you run, not walk, to this bakery. This landmark Danish bakery opened up in 1974, and the owner can still be found baking in the back about five days a week. This bakery is famous for its *kringles,* layers of buttery crust, filled with almond paste and raisins, topped with sugar and sliced almonds, and twisted into a pretzel shape. They also have a large selection of marzipan cakes that you can custom order, a fantastic selection of breads, and rows of additional pastries and cookies.

Mighty-O Donuts, 2110 N. 55th St., Seattle, WA 98103; (206) 547-0335; Wallingford; www.mightyo.com. There is no way you can call doughnuts healthy and get away with it, but there are ways to make them less unhealthy. Mighty-O makes certified-organic doughnuts, with no chemical preservatives, no coloring or artificial flavors, and no animal-derived ingredients. Some flavors include nutty chocolate, French toast, lemon poppy, chocolate raspberry, and ever-changing seasonal flavors. The Mighty-O Donut shop has a nice seating space in front of an open window for the closet people watchers. They carry mini doughnuts for those who want to mix and match. Doughnuts are half price (75 cents) between 4 and 5 p.m., but the variety is limited. You can also find Mighty-O Donuts at local cafes and specialty stores that carry organic products.

Minoo Bakery, 12518 Lake City Way Northeast, Seattle, WA 98125; (206) 306-2229; Lake City; www.minoobakery.com. This Persian bakery is a bit of a drive from downtown, but it deserves a visit if you like to discover different flavors. You will find cream puffs, Danishes, and baklava complemented by Persian touches such as pistachio, rosewater, and cardamom. Try the *Naan-e-Nokhochi*, a flower-shaped chickpea cookie dipped in chocolate that melts in your mouth. Other delights include *Naan-e Berenji*, and almond-coconut cookies. If you like your desserts really sweet then you will like the *zulbia*, deep-fried dough circles that are soaked in honey—a Persian version of the American funnel cake. The cookies are priced reasonably ($5.99 or $6.99 a pound), so make up a box with a few of every kind. While you are in the neighborhood, you can pick up authentic home-cooked Persian food to go or dine in at **Pacific Market,** a no-frills Persian grocery shop and restaurant (12332 Lake City Way Northeast, Seattle, WA 98125; Lake City; 206-363-8639).

Molly Moon's Homemade Ice Cream, 1622 N. 45th St., Seattle, WA 98103; (206) 547-5105; Wallingford; and 917 E. Pine St., Seattle, WA 98122; (206) 708-7947; Capitol Hill; www.molly moonicecream.com. Molly Moon may be the perfect name for a neighborhood ice-cream shop, but I'm sure this was not in her parents' plans. Born to a hippie couple (yes, Molly Moon Neitzel is her real name), Molly worked in politics and the music industry before deciding to open her own ice-cream shop. Molly uses locally grown and organic ingredients when possible: dairy from Monroe and Duvall, Washington; organic fruit for toppings; and Tahuya River Apiaries honey, harvested from the foothills of the Olympic Mountains. Molly Moon's flavors include balsamic strawberry, Theo Chocolate, Scout mint, salted caramel, Starburst, and many more. If you like your ice cream extra creamy, this is the place. Just be prepared to wait in line, rain or shine. Follow the ice-cream truck on Twitter: @mollymoon.

Peak's Frozen Custard Cafe, 1026 N.E. 65th St., A101, Seattle, WA 98115; (206) 588-2701; Roosevelt; www.peaksfrozencustard .com. When you are in the mood for a simple and creamy dessert, frozen custard is a great bet. Peak's locally sourced frozen custard is churned quickly at very low temperatures in a specialized machine, thus avoiding large ice crystal formation and the introduction of air. It has a higher concentration of egg yolk but lower butterfat than ice cream. Peak's has hundreds of creative flavors but offers only 4 each day: chocolate, vanilla, a flavor of the day, and a flavor of the week. Since custard needs to be served fresh, they ensure you get fresh custard every time by keeping the flavor variety light. If you want to choose your flavor in advance, be sure to check the Flavor Forecast on the website. This place also has house-made cakes, Lighthouse Roasters espresso, sandwiches, free Wi-Fi, a fireplace, and a beautiful kids area equipped with toys and games.

Simply Desserts, 3421 Fremont Ave. North, Seattle, WA 98103; (206) 633-2671; Fremont; www.simplydessertsseattle.com. No name can better describe this 20-seat cake shop that has been around for 30 years. It's the kind of place you go for a slice of cake after dinner or when you want to order a cheesecake for a special occasion. You will find freshly baked cakes like Kahlua-swirl cheesecake, lemon cheesecake, Chocolate Raspberry Rhapsody, and other decadent flavors. The most sought-after are the strawberry–white choco-late and the chocolate–white chocolate cakes. Sometimes, you just have to keep it sweet and simple.

Tall Grass Bakery, 5907 24th Ave. Northwest, Seattle, WA 98107; (206) 706-0991; Ballard; www.tallgrassbakery.com. Side-by-side bakeries, how dangerous! Tall Grass Bakery is located right next to **Cafe Besalu** (see page 2), one of the best French bakeries around. But that's okay, because Besalu is where you have your buttery croissant, and Tall Grass is where you pick up the baguette that you are going to have for dinner. This artisan bread bakery has items like hearty and heavily seeded rye bread, oat and honey bread, pumpernickel, cherry pumpernickel, and olive *fougasse*. They are open from 9 a.m. to 7 p.m., 7 days a week and have an extended selection on weekends. Don't miss the raisin-pecan granola.

Theo Chocolate, 3400 Phinney Ave. North, Seattle, WA 98103; (206) 632-5100; Fremont; www.theochocolate.com. If you smell chocolate on your walk near the Fremont Bridge, you're only a hop, skip, and jump away from this showroom equipped with samples galore. Theo Chocolate has put Seattle on the map for being the only certified-organic, fair-traded bean-to-bar factory in the United States, with Oprah giving them her A-OK in the February 2008 issue of her magazine. The fantasy-flavor line consists of combinations like bread and chocolate; coconut curry; Chai tea; fig, fennel, and almond; and nib brittle. They carry single-origin chocolates for those with a darker preference, as well as handmade confections, caramels, and vegan dark truffles. Theo offers chocolate tours all day long for only $6, and they are open 7 days a week. Reservations are required. When you call, make sure to ask if there will be production on the day of your visit, or you might miss out on watching the machines in action. Bring your camera because chocolate-covered faces and hairnets make for a great photo.

Three Girls Bakery; 6209 15th Ave. Northwest, Seattle, WA 98107; (206) 420-7613; Ballard. For a full description see the Downtown listing, p. 107.

Trophy Cupcakes and Party, 1815 N. 45th St., Suite 209, Seattle, WA 98103; (206) 632-7020; Wallingford; www.trophy cupcakes.com. (See website for additional locations.) Co-owner, Jennifer Shea's love for baking started at the ripe age of 6 when she began baking for parties and family gatherings. Later in life she and her husband, Michael Williamson, decided to open the first Trophy Cupcakes in Wallingford in 2007. The cupcake couple now own three successful locations. Trophy is known for its custom-made cupcakes, baked from scratch every day. Varieties include choices like Valrhona chocolate cupcake, pure Madagascar bourbon vanilla cupcake, and the popularity-contest winner: red velvet. If you are looking for more daring flavors, choose by the day of the week; opt for Monday's snickerdoodle or Sunday's Chai cardamom. Jennifer will custom design cupcakes for events and parties, and if you are craving cupcakes but are too lazy to go out, just call, because this place delivers.

Bubble Tea

Have you noticed students walking around town clenching clear plastic cups with gigantic straws? This may seem like a milkshake but this drink is bubble tea, a sweet beverage originating from Taiwan, made of tea and mixed with fruit or milk. These teas are shaken leaving a foam on top giving them their name, Bubble Tea. The drinks contain tapioca pearls known as "boba" that have a springy almost gummy candy–like texture, adding an element of fun to a refreshing and filling drink that is just as good a snack as it is a dessert. There are many variations; with milk or without, mixed with green tea or black tea, and tapioca alternatives like lychee jelly, coconut jelly, and more. Where to get it?

Shinka Tea (4727 University Way, N.E., Seattle, WA 98105; 206-522-8424; University District; www.shinkatea.com)

Yunnie Bubble Tea (4511 University Way N.E., Seattle, WA 98105; 206-547-9648; University District)

Pochi Tea Station (5014 University Way N.E., Seattle, WA 98105; 206-529 8388; University District)

Oasis Tea Zone (519 6th Ave. S., Seattle, WA 98104; 206-447-8098; Chinatown/International District)

Gossip (651 S. King St., Seattle, WA 98104; 206-624-5402; Chinatown/ International District; gossip-tea.com)

Bobachine (1514 4th Ave., Seattle, WA 98101; 206-447-2622; Downtown; www.bobachine.com)

The Confectionery, 4608 26th Ave. Northeast, Seattle, WA 98105; (206) 523-1443; University District; www.theconfectionery .com. This candy shop, located in University Village, has a classic old-fashioned feel, with colorful bags of candies everywhere to satiate your voracious sweet tooth. They have handmade chocolates and truffles, jelly beans in all colors, jawbreakers, gummy candy, and a nice selection of confections lining the walls in clear jars. Swing by and pick up a few bags of sweets for a friend's birthday or as a treat for yourself.

Continental Halal and Spices, 7819 Aurora Ave. North, Seattle, WA 98103; (206) 706-0326; Greenwood. Next time you plan an Indian feast and need ingredients, drop by this specialty store to get everything Indian your heart desires—fresh curry leaves, spices of every kind, ghee, and more. This market carries imported products from all over India, as well as Mediterranean and Arabic products. They sell local halal meat, including fresh goat and lamb. Before the weekend, you will find some desserts on the counter such as *jalebi*, deep-fried batter soaked in sugary syrup; *rasgulla*, cheese balls in a syrup; and other Indian specialties.

Fresh Fish Company, 2364 N.W. 80th St., Seattle, WA 98117; (206) 782-1632; Ballard. With a name like Fresh Fish, you have a reputation to uphold, and this family-run shop has been living up to its name for over 25 years. Ballard's fish shop has loads of fresh seafood, with items like lingcod, halibut, prawns, sea scallops, king salmon, and more. The staff is made up of true fishmongers with years of experience and the willingness to help you decide. They also have shellfish, marinated pork and beef, and their own specialty: alderwood–smoked salmon. In the same shop, you will find the famous Cascioppo Brothers meats and sausages.

Metropolitan Market, 5250 40th Ave. Northeast, Seattle, WA 98105; (206) 938-6600; Sand Point; www.metropolitan-market .com. For a full description see the Central listing, p. 59.

Pasta & Co, 4622 26th Ave. Northeast, Seattle, WA 98105; (206) 523-8594; University District; www.pastaco.com. For a full description see the Central listing, p. 60.

PCC Natural Markets, 600 N. 34th St., Seattle, WA 98103; (206) 632-6811; Fremont; (206) 525-3586; www.pccnaturalmarkets.com. (See website for additional locations.) What started off as a food-buying club for 15 families in 1953 has progressed into a natural-foods co-operative owned by the 45,000 members who, together with many nonmembers, reap the benefits of healthy, local, natural products. With multiple locations all over the greater Seattle area, PCC provides a wide variety of good-for-you merchandise, adhering to strict guidelines preventing unhealthy additives and supporting local and sustainable movements and products. They have a large selection of house-made salads and foods as well as fresh breads, organic produce, wines, and a convenient bulk section. They also run a program (Kid Picks) that points out healthy kids' snacks and offers a free piece of fruit for children under 12—a lifesaver when your child is having a tantrum—which makes shopping here an extremely enjoyable experience. This is an ideal place to shop if you have allergies or food intolerances.

Picnic, 6801 Greenwood Ave. North, Unit 113A, Seattle, WA 98103; (206) 453-5867; Phinney Ridge; www.picnicseattle.com. While Seattle weather may often drive the picnics indoors, Picnic offers choices that would make a great spread at any location. They have a wide selection of tasty to-go foods, from charcuterie and cheese to house-made items like corned beef, pâté, soups, and salads. This modern specialty food-and-wine shop has it all, including over 350 wines from small producers, and condiments and products like Rancho Gordo Heirloom Beans, Boat Street Pickles, and artisanal honey from local **Ballard Bee Company** (www .ballardbeecompany.com/Ballard_Bee_Company). There is indoor seating, and outdoor seating is available when weather permits. On Thursday, they have themed wine tastings between 5:30 and 7:30 p.m. for just $8. They also offer catering for private events.

Frost Doughnuts

First, let me warn you. This is a long drive. But hey, if you are a hardcore doughnut lover, then nothing will come between you and this mouthwatering pastry bliss made fresh daily in these harmoniously creative flavors like Bourbon Caramel Pecan, Chocolate Caramel Truffle, and the intense must-try Smoky Bacon-Maple Bar. If you have enough willpower to follow them on Twitter: @frostology then be prepared to get a morning update with their daily flavors and don't blame me if you catch yourself licking your fingers or the steering wheel in the wee morning hours. Check their website because a greater Seattle location should be coming soon! **Frost Doughnuts,** 15421 Main St., Ste. H102, Mill Creek, WA 98012; (425) 379-2600; www.frostology.com.

Savour, 2242 N.W. Market St., Seattle, WA 98107; (206) 789-0775; Ballard; www.savourspecialtyfoods.com. If you love browsing specialty food shops for inspiration, then this is the place for you. The friendly, welcoming staff will answer all your questions. They have a large assortment of cheeses and specialty chocolates, balsamic oils, vinegars, sauces, and many other foods and spices. Regular wine tastings are held in the charming tasting area, where they also have seating for customers dining in. Special events for small groups can be accommodated on request. The sandwich case offers quick lunches like the recommended Jamón y Queso, which consists of imported Manchego cheese, Serrano ham, and fig jam. They are closed Mon.

The Shop Agora, 6417-A Phinney Ave. North, Seattle, WA 98103; (206) 782-5551; Phinney Ridge; www .theshopagora.com. Nikos and Alexis, the owners of this Greek specialty shop, combined their passion for food and wine to open this neighborhood gem. Nikos, a native of Greece with a hospitality background in the food and wine industry, and Alexis, a nutritionist, handpick the highest-quality products to showcase in their shop. This place is proof that good things come in small packages, with a huge selection of Greek wines, endless varieties of condiments, balsamic vinegars, oils, crackers, and chocolates all packed into this tiny shop. Pick up some of the competitively priced kalamata olives that they brine themselves. They have a selection of Mediterranean gift baskets with gluten-free options that can be ordered and delivered anywhere in Seattle.

Trader Joe's, 4609 14th Ave. Northwest, Seattle, WA 98107; (206) 783-0498; Ballard; www.traderjoes.com. (See website for additional locations.) For a full description see the Central listing, p. 62.

University Seafood & Poultry, 1317 N.E. 47th St., Seattle, WA 98105; (206) 632-3900 or (206) 632-3700; University District; http://universityseafoodandpoultry.lbu.com. Four generations of the Erickson family have been serving the community with the freshest fish and a full spectrum of seafood from mussels, clams, salmon, halibut, cod, crab—and the list goes on. They also have caviar, poultry, game meats and game birds, and more. Loyal customers have been coming here for over 65 years because of the attention to details, quality product, customer service, and their purist approach to food. They are closed on Sun.

Whole Foods Market, 1026 N.E. 64th St., Seattle, WA 98115; (206) 985-1500; Roosevelt; www.wholefoodsmarket.com. For a full description see the Central listing, p. 62.

Food Lovers' Faves

Art of the Table, 1054 N. 39th St., Seattle, WA 98103; (206) 282-0942; Wallingford/Fremont; www.artofthetable.net; $$$$. This is too much of a treasure not to share. Chef Dustin Ronspies welcomes you into this compact and homey house filled with small tables and seating in unexpected places: a duo seat overlooking the kitchen, two on a window, and a communal table for the art of sharing. You'll find local ingredients combined perfectly for optimal flavor with unexpected combinations. Monday happy hours are not to be missed; supper clubs are private dinner parties with prix-fixe menus at $55 for 4 courses; and everything here is a work of art.

A Taste of India, 5517 Roosevelt Way Northeast, Seattle, WA 98105; (206) 528-1575; University District; www.tasteofindia seattle.com; $$. Don't come in the door looking for an Indian buffet because this restaurant has none of that. This house-turned-restaurant has cooked-to-order Indian food, an ambitious menu, and fresh bread at your fingertips. Appetizers are generous, with plates like the Taste of India Delight, which includes vegetable samosa, vegetable pakora, chicken tikka, lamb kebab, and a duo of chutneys. Choose from an extensive list of tandoori cuisine, masalas, or curries. The menu also has Mediterranean dishes and salads. Do not miss the perfectly spiced, never-ending Chai; refills are on the house.

Bastille, 5307 Ballard Ave. Northwest, Seattle, WA 98117; (206) 453-5014; Ballard; www.bastilleseattle.com; $$$. You might think charming your date is all about fancy chocolate, but in this locavore-loving city, dinner in a restaurant that grows its own herbs on the roof will surely score you a second date or at the least a peck on the cheek. This neighborhood French cafe and bistro is a happening spot in the Ballard neighborhood with classy French decor and a rich chocolate-colored wood bar. Daily happy hour is a great deal from 4:30 to 6 p.m. and again Sun through Thurs, 10 p.m. to 1 a.m. Recommended: salad verte, in which the ingredients come straight from the rooftop garden, and the burger d'agneau, a lamb burger with harissa, aioli, arugula, pickled shallot, and frites.

Cantinetta, 3650 Wallingford Ave. North, Seattle, WA 98103; (206) 632-1000; Wallingford; www.cantinettaseattle.com; $$. (See website for additional locations.) This warm Italian hideaway is located in the middle of a residential neighborhood. The place is endearingly romantic while vivacious and lively. The half-open kitchen, dark wood tables, and beautiful chandeliers give it a warm, cozy mood. Everything here is handmade, from the bread to the pasta, with an emphasis on seasonal and local ingredients. On winter nights, seek warmth at this enchanting refuge; summer evenings are great for dining outside. Recommended: pancetta-wrapped dates and ricotta gnocchi.

Caspian Grill, 5517 University Way Northeast, Seattle, WA 98105; (206) 524-3434; University District; www.caspiangrill.com; $$. When asking my Persian friends about their favorite places to eat, the first answer I always get is "in my mother's home," and the second is always this restaurant. The restaurant has a warm atmosphere, but the food is even warmer; the kebabs, slow-cooked stews, and nutty basmati rice provide a taste of home away from home for many of my friends. The *fesenjan*—tender chicken thighs in pomegranate sauce with ground walnuts—is a local favorite. Choose one of the platters to get the full experience, or start with some pita and one of the flavorful spreads. Call in on Friday and

Saturday nights to find out if there will be belly-dancing performances. A new location is opening at 1806 136th Place in Bellevue. Visit the website for details.

Delancey, 1415 N.W. 70th St.; Seattle, WA 98117; (206) 838-1960; Ballard; www.delanceyseattle.com; $$. In the good ol' days, love stories were conceived in bowling alleys, movie theaters, and pizza parlors, but renowned Seattle food blogger Molly Wizenberg and her husband, Brandon Pettit, tell a more modern love story. They met through her blog, Orangette (http://orangette.blogspot .com) and ended up opening a pizza parlor together. Delancey is small, rustic, and wildly romantic. It's focused on making thin-crust pizzas with locally sourced ingredients and creating an environment of simplicity and warmth. As with all good things, they come to those who wait: Lines here are long; in many cases over an hour. Come in and get on the list and grab a drink at a nearby bar while you wait. On Wednesday, Thursday, and Friday, drop by early between 5 and 6 p.m. Saturday is frequently busy at all times, but on Sunday, 8 p.m. is a good time to squeeze in. They don't take reservations except for 6 or more, so round up some friends and book the table. Coming in an hour before you want to eat would be the ideal way to go.

El Camino, 607 N. 35th St., Seattle, WA 98103; (206) 632-7303; Fremont; www.elcaminorestaurant.com; $$. As much as I love down-home Mexican food in an easy-going setting, sometimes you want the down-home style with a little fashion. El Camino is all that. It is where you go for a special dinner or to catch up with an old friend at the bar in a modern space with colorful designs, lanterns, and mirrors. Separate dining areas offer different dining atmospheres. Grab a seat in the beautiful closed patio area or in the romantic dining room. Enjoy traditional and contemporary cuisine with menu items like tamales, gorditas, and enchiladas en mole.

Elemental @ Gasworks, 3309 Wallingford Ave. North, Seattle, WA 98103; (206) 547-2317; Wallingford; www.elementalatgasworks .com; $$$$. Adventurous and spontaneous eaters take note: Prepare to surrender your inhibitions at the door of this unique restaurant. Phred Westfall and Laurie Riedeman are known for putting together special evenings where they decide on the courses and leave you with an element of surprise. Phred's extensive wine knowledge covers everything from the staples to the esoteric, and his deft touch in food-and-wine pairing expresses that. Arrive without any preconceived notions. The food will be placed in front of you, and you won't know what it is until you try it. Side effects will include perfect wine pairings with every course and no substitutions. They don't take reservations and like things their way. Be prepared to wait in line; no parties over 6. Hours are from 5 p.m. to midnight. A vegetarian tasting menu is available. The price is $40 for 5 courses, $80 with cocktail and wine pairings with every course. If this whole dictatorship way of eating isn't your thing, go next door to **Elemental Next Door,** the wine bar where you can get snacks and wines by the glass, half bottle, or full bottles. *Note:* You might not find this place at first glance but it exists; just keep looking.

Flying Squirrel Pizza, 5433 Ballard Ave. Northwest, Seattle, WA 98107; (206) 784-4880; www.flyingsquirrelpizza.com; $. This pizzeria is located inside the **Sunset Tavern** (www.sunsettavern .com) and serves pizza from 5 to 9 p.m.; after 9 p.m. there is a cover entrance for shows. For a full description see the South listing, p. 159.

Golden Beetle, 1744 NW Market Street, Seattle, WA 98107; (206) 706-2977; Ballard; www.golden-beetle.com; $$$. This much-welcome second restaurant from Chef Maria Hines of **Tilth** (see p. 35) gives palates a new sense of exploration with robust spices and earthy flavors of the Eastern Mediterranean. The menu reveals influences from Chef Hines' travels to Turkey, Greece, Lebanon, and Egypt as well as inspiration from Israel, Tunisia, Algeria, and Morocco. She mixes those influences with her dedication to local farmers and foragers of certified organic cuisine. The bar is slightly larger than the dining room, but there is a flow throughout that encourages lively conversation in a vivacious atmosphere. Tasting menus are available. Happy hour is Sun, Tues, and Thurs from 5 to 6 p.m. and 10 p.m. to midnight. A late night menu is offered Sun,

Tues, and Thurs from 10 p.m. to midnight, and Fri and Sat from 10:30 p.m. to 1 a.m. See Chef Maria Hines's recipe for **Chocolate Ganache Cakes** on p. 209.

Gorgeous George's, .7719 Greenwood Ave. North, Seattle, WA 98103; (206) 783-0116; Greenwood; www.gorgeousgeorges.com; $$. If you like Middle Eastern food, then you will love it here. White tablecloths may adorn the tables, but this place is surprisingly casual. Chef George swings out of the kitchen, takes your order, and whips up a Mediterranean feast. Start your meal with the fluffy pita and homemade hummus; the hummus is topped with olive oil and *za'atar,* a spice blend made of sumac, sesame seeds, and other spices. The entrees are generous enough for two, but order more and take home the rest. Open for lunch Wed through Sat and dinner daily, but make sure to check the website for hours because it closes as early as 9 p.m., and George takes a siesta between lunch and dinner.

Homegrown Sandwiches, 3416 Fremont Ave. North, Seattle, WA 98103; (206) 453-5232; Fremont; www.eathomegrown.com; $. For a full description see the Central listing, p. 70.

Joule, 1913 N. 45th St.; Seattle, WA 98103; (206) 632-1913; Wallingford; www.joulerestaurant.com; $$. The husband-and-wife culinary duo behind this creative French-Korean restaurant is responsible for a superstar play on flavor and fine dining in a most comfortable, unpretentious atmosphere. Chefs Seif Chirchi and Rachel Yang have a talent for combining unique Asian ingredients with comfort food, a pendulum of flavors and surprising combinations. You might find menu items like smoked tofu and honshimeji confit with soy-truffle vinaigrette, or Joule BBQ—a short-rib steak, homemade chili sausage with grilled Napa cabbage kimchee and a squash chowchow. One of the highlights of the summer is the Joule Urban Barbecue Series: every Sunday there is a different city theme with places like Marseille; France; and Oaxaca, Mexico. Summer dining menu includes a hot dish and a "picnic table" with a selection of cold dishes, desserts, and bread for only $18 for adults and $10 for kids.

Kisaku, 2101 N. 55th St., #100, Seattle, WA 98103; (206) 545-9050; Wallingford/Green Lake; www.kisaku.com/kisaku; $$. You probably wouldn't know about this place unless you lived in the neighborhood or were referred by Japanese friends or hard-core sushi connoisseurs. The love for this place is apparent when you see how packed it gets; sushi purists come here for the freshest sushi and the traditional, seasonal offerings. For the complete sushi experience, order *omakase* on the bar; which means you let the chef send out his choice of the best. Reservations recommended. To keep up with what comes in daily, follow Kisaku on Twitter: @kisakusushi. Just be wary; you might find yourself dashing in for lunch when you should otherwise be working.

La Carta de Oxaca, 5431 Ballard Ave. Northwest, Seattle, WA 98107; (206) 782-8722; Ballard; www.lacartadeoaxaca.com; $. Seattleites may have different tastes in food, but when it comes to Mexican, food locals will agree on this favorite. La Carta's home-made tortilla chips and serve-yourself salsa bar are a sure sign that delicious food is on the way. The mole dishes are in a league of their own, as are any dishes that include the homemade torti-llas. The surroundings are fast paced with quick, bouncing staff, pumping music, and a lively, positive vibe. Waits are long, but nothing that a margarita at the bar couldn't fix.

La Isla, 2320 N.W. Market St., Seattle, WA 98107; (206) 789-0516; Ballard; www .laislaseattle.com; $$. Puerto Rican res-taurants don't come easy around here. This is one of two in the entire city; the other, **El Pilón** (see p. 158), is in Columbia City. This res-taurant and bar is lively, tasty, and relatively inexpen-sive—especially for lunch. It's a great choice for a drink with some friends or some loitering on the summer patio. Be sure to start with the fried turnovers called empanadillas and one of their specialty cocktails like the "10 Cane Mojito". You will find plates like Pernil Sliders made with house-made, oven-braised, and hand-pulled pork. Catch the happy hour daily from 3 to 6 p.m. or 10 p.m. to midnight, when appetizers are half price. It is a great place in Ballard to pull up a bar stool and watch the hipsters and bicyclists peddle by.

The Monkey Bridge, 1723 N.W. Market St, Seattle; WA 98107; (206) 297-6048; Ballard; $. Everybody needs a place to pop in for a casual dinner and this Vietnamese restaurant really hits the spot. The wooden furniture, red lanterns and minimalist decor create a zen atmosphere and the crisp fresh flavors come through in the food. You will find a an extensive menu with items ranging from salad rolls, noodle dishes, rice dishes, and salads to the Vietnamese Baguette sandwiches known as *Bánh Mì*. The combination of tasty food and good value make this an easy option for take-out.

Mr. Gyro's, 8411 Greenwood Ave. North, Seattle, WA 98103; (206) 706-7472; Greenwood; www.mrgyroseattle.com; $. (See website for additional location.) The lines out the door of this tiny fast-food hole-in-wall are sure signs that gyros are the way to warm up on a chilly day. Watch the spit-roasted beef and lamb twirling before you, while the friendly staff behind the counter bops to the beat of the blasting club music. Take your massive pita stuffed with meat and vegetables to-go, since space is tight. Whether you get the falafel, *shawarma,* or the gyro, just know that your wallet won't suffer, though you may have to open a button on your pants.

Pam's Kitchen, 5000 University Way Northeast, Seattle, WA 98105; (206) 696-7010; University District; www.pams-kitchen .com; $$. If you haven't had Trinidadian food, get yourself here, quick. This restaurant is not the kind of place you come when you're in a hurry, and owner Pam will explain that it's because all the food is cooked to order, she serves it all fresh with love. The brief menu offers roti, a doughy flatbread with your choice of curried meat and lightly curried potatoes, garbanzo beans, and salad. The seasoned potato patties known as aloo pies are a scrumptious appetizer, and ambitious spice lovers must not deny themselves the famous jerk chicken. Vegans and vegetarian options are available as well. Do check the hours before you go, because even on the days it opens for lunch, it seems to close in between lunch and dinner.

Paseo, 4225 Fremont Ave. North, Seattle, WA 98103; (206) 545-7440; Fremont; www.paseoseattle.com; $. (See website for additional location.) Hands down, this eatery has one of the best sandwiches in town. The hole-in-the-wall Caribbean restaurant with a Cuban influence doesn't have a decoration in sight, but the food—including a drippingly messy sandwich—will instantly transport you to tropical sandy beaches. Order the Cuban Roast, roasted pork shoulder in a secret Paseo marinade sandwiched in a toasted baguette with aioli, cilantro, lettuce, caramelized onions, and jalapeños for that extra kick. If you have the patience for an upgrade, wait an extra 10 minutes, and you could be the lucky consumer of the Midnight Cuban Press, similar to the former except with ham and cheese and hotly pressed. Order the corn on the cob, slathered in garlic and butter. If you can bear to walk away from the sandwiches, there are also non-sandwich items that are reputably tasty. Be prepared to wait in line. Make this the place for days when you want to order and take out. *Note:* They only take cash.

Plaka Estiatorio, 5407 20th Ave. Northwest, Seattle, WA 98107; (206) 829-8934; Ballard; www.plakaballard.com; $$. There aren't that many Greek restaurants in town, so when you find one that you like, you hold on and you don't let go. Plaka fills the Ballard niche for Greek hospitality and authentic dishes in a rustic setting. You will find menu items like *mezedes* (small plates) with octopus braised in herbs with lemon and olive oil, or spanakopita (phyllo pastry with spinach and feta), souvlaki, grilled lamb chops, and more. Authentic wooden tables and chairs set the mood for this comforting family-friendly restaurant. Open for lunch and dinner. Recommended: *marithes* (fried wild smelts) with skordalia or the *horta* (braised seasonal greens with lemon).

Revel, 403 N. 36th St., Seattle, WA, 98103; (206) 547-2040; Fremont; www.revelseattle.com; $$. If discovering new takes on Asian comfort and bold flavors make your heart tick, then let yourself revel in the creativeness of this modern, warm space with a large open kitchen created by Chef Rachel Yang and Seif Chirchi, the duo behind Wallingford's beloved Korean-French restaurant known as Joule. Here you will find enough style for a casual din-din with your lover or a night out with the kids. Menu items like pancakes with pork belly, kimchi, and bean sprouts or dumplings filled with chorizo, jicama, and cilantro are ideal for sharing. Order with a group from each menu category (noodles, rice, dumplings, and pancakes), but don't leave without dessert: house-made ice-cream sandwiches. For late night drinks, sit at the bar attached by the name of **Quoin** where you can try cocktails and infused soju; Korea's distilled beverage that resembles vodka.

Señor Moose Cafe, 5242 N.W. Leary Ave., Seattle, WA 98107; (206) 784-5568; Ballard; www.senormoose.com; $$. A Mexican-themed franchise with a similar name might come to mind, but this place couldn't be any more different. What started off as an American breakfast restaurant by the original name of Cafe Moose quickly turned into a Mexican gem when owner Kathleen Andersen began introducing Mexican fare to the brunch menu. Now, Señor Moose is a Ballard favorite, with eclectic food from the different states of Mexico cooked in the style called *"comida tipica,"* which is, as Kathleen explains, "cooking found in central plateau Mexico's *fondas* [inns] and backroom kitchens." Brunch favorites include *huevos ahogados* from Mexico City, which are poached eggs in a delicious spicy tomato broth with poblano chile strips. For dinner, popular dishes are *camarones enchipotlados* (shrimp sautéed in a creamy chipotle sauce and served with black beans and rice) and *alambres*, a variation on a dish from Oaxaca, which consists of house-made chorizo, bacon, and *machaca* (shredded, crispy beef) all grilled together with poblanos and green peppers, topped with cheese and fresh green salsa, and served with refried beans. The restaurant also features several moles, such as *mole negro tlaxcalteca* (from Tlaxcala) and *mole colarodito de Tututepec* (from Oaxaca), among others.

Shiku Sushi, 5310 Ballard Ave. Northwest, Seattle, WA 98107; (206) 588-2151; Ballard; www.shikusushi.com; $$. This posh Ballard sushi restaurant and cocktail bar has a nice atmosphere, comfortable benches, and two bar seating areas—one traditional bar and one sushi bar that gives you a view of the chefs, some sporting black fedoras, while you dine. In addition to a sushi menu, they have an *Isakaya* menu; small plate, snack items like vegetable tempura, fried stuffed jalapeños filled with snow crab and cream cheese, and Agedashi tofu. The happy hour is an excellent deal with a substantial assortment of food items and drinks. Check the website for hours.

Staple & Fancy Mercantile, 4739 Ballard Ave. Northwest, Seattle, WA 98107; (206) 789-1200; Ballard; www.ethanstowellres taurants.com/stapleandfancy; $$. With a name like this, you might not imagine that a restaurant would occupy this spot, but lo and behold, it is the latest from the Ethan Stowell Restaurants group. This early 20th-century building was once home to a mercantile that offered both staple and fancy products for Ballard residents.

Open for dinner 7 days a week, you can find fabulous, clean Italian flavors, seasonal selections, and hand-crafted pastas. Grab a spot at the bar and you'll likely catch Chef Ethan Stowell in action, or opt for a table in the industrial-style dining room with its high ceilings, exposed ducts, and hand-painted brick walls. The way to order is the chef's choice dining experience, where a 4-course family-style menu will be crafted for you by the chef. See Chef Ethan Stowell's recipe for **Gnocchetti with Pancetta, Spring Onions & English Peas** on p. 196.

Stumbling Goat Bistro, 6722 Greenwood Ave. North, Seattle, WA 98103; (206) 784-3535; Greenwood/Phinney; www.stumbling goatbistro.com; $$$. This neighborhood restaurant is undoubtedly Seattle with its minimalist decor, local art on the walls, and customers sporting a large range of attire (from jeans to dressy). The menu is subtly ambitious with sustainable, organic Northwest ingredients and fresh flavors. Flipping through the menu will reveal a list of all the local producers, from the farmers to the bakeries, identifying a restaurant that supports its community. You will find seasonal items that rotate often, like local Thundering Hooves New York steak, pork chops, or short ribs and the recommended pan-roasted Mad Hatcher Farm chicken with roasted-garlic confit. Happy hour is a good option for some snacks and drinks with items ranging from $3 to $6.

Tilth, 1411 N. 45th St., Seattle, WA 98103; (206) 633-0801; Wallingford; www.tilthrestaurant.com; $$$. In a little green house, there is a farm-to-table restaurant called Tilth, with huge ideas, cutting-edge flavors, and Chef Maria Hines, who won the Food Network's Iron Chef Competition as well as a critically acclaimed James Beard Award for Best Chef of the Northwest. The food is New American cuisine prepared with either wild or organic ingredients from local farmers; it is a certified organic dining establishment. Interesting plays on flavors and textures make Tilth a special place for the adventurous palate with a craving for fresh, wholesome food. Menu items come in two sizes so you can order a larger portion. If you catch the mini duck burgers (with fingerling potatoes and homemade ketchup and hot mustard) on the menu, you'll want to get them. See Chef Maria Hines's recipe for **Chocolate Ganache Cakes** on p. 209.

Tutta Bella, 4411 Stone Way North, Seattle, WA, 98103; (206) 633-3800, Wallingford; www.tuttabellapizza.com; $$. For a full description see the South listing, p. 163.

Veraci Pizza, 500 N.W. Market St., Seattle, WA 98107; (206) 525-1813; Ballard; www.veracipizza.com; $. Veraci gained its popularity while participating in the local farmers' markets around town. Who could resist a wood-fired oven smack in

ROAD TRIP: INN AT LANGLEY

Fast-paced city life has its perks: restaurants everywhere, grocery stores on the corner, and a vibrant energy that keeps you moving. But on occasion, the country calls.

For urban Seattleites, country living seems a world away, but only an hour and 20 minutes from downtown will take you to a relaxing get- away. A short trip to Whidbey Island's **Inn at Langley** (400 1st St., Langley, WA 98260; 360-221-3033; www.innatlangley.com) provides the perfect respite for gathering your thoughts—curl up with a book in one of the inn's guest rooms and listen to the water lap the rocky shore, or stroll the storybook town of Langley and make friends with the shopkeepers.

A 40-minute drive from downtown and a relaxing ferry ride will get you there. Inn manager and chef Matt Costello's memorable six-course dinner is an experience in itself, set against the wood-accented dining room with its stunning double-sided river-rock fireplace and display kitchen. Costello begins each meal with a brief description of the day's ingredients and where they're from—usually over 80 percent from right there on Whidbey. And his cooking is a dazzling partnership of hyperlocal ingredients and modernist technique.

the middle of a market full of produce and artisan cheeses? Eventually they started a traveling pizza catering service for events and opened a Ballard location. This paper-thin pizza crust has a chewy and crunchy texture topped with high-quality local ingredi-

Dinner at 7 p.m. on Friday and Saturday is $85 per person, not including tax, wine, and gratuity. Wine pairings are an additional $65 to $80, or choose something from the inn's impressive cellar. And if it's just a day trip you're after, a Sunday visit without an overnight is doable, as dinner starts at 6 p.m., providing ample time to catch the ferry home. In the summer, dinner is served at 7 p.m. on Thursday as well.

Other must-visit stops in Langley include **Prima Bistro** (201½ 1st St., Langley, WA 98260; 360-221-4060; www.primabistro.com/) for cocktails and great French-inspired fare; **Useless Bay Coffee Company** (121 2nd St., Langley, WA 98260; 360-221-4515; www.uselessbaycoffee.com/) for terrific fresh-roasted coffee; the adorable **Clyde Theater** (217 1st St., Langley, WA 98260; 360-221-5525; www.theclyde.net/) to catch a flick; and any of the four distinctive bookshops when you finish the book you brought and need another. More about Langley as well as other lodging opportunities can be found at www.visitlangley.com.

For directions to Langley, visit www.langleywa.org/documents/directions-seattle-to-langley.pdf.

ents. Expect pizzas like the Luna Rosa, with savory red sauce, fresh mozzarella, Cascioppo Brothers' Italian sausage, salami, and roasted peppers, or the Salume (pepperoni, salami, black olives, provolone, garlic, and olive oil). One slice of this light pizza just tickles your taste buds, so you might want to double up or order a salad on the side. For desserts, house-made gelato and sorbetto come in flavors like Theo Chocolate, hazelnut, and vibrant fruit flavors.

Via Tribunali, 4303 Fremont Ave. North, Seattle, WA 98103; (206) 547-2144; Fremont; www.viatribunali.net; $$. For a full description see the Central listing, p. 84.

Volterra, 5411 Ballard Ave. Northwest, Seattle, WA 98107; (206) 789-5100; Ballard; www.volterrarestaurant.com; $$$. Owners Michelle Quisenberry and Don Curtiss met through mutual friend and local Chef Kathy Casey and together they began a love story and Volterra, a restaurant that unites ingredients from the Northwest and Italy. Reminders of their wedding decorate the room and its beautiful chandeliers and romantic atmosphere. The pastas are hearty and handmade, and paired with interesting cuts of meat; the menu includes items like orecchiette pasta with lamb ragu, and baked gnocchi with wild-boar sausage. Brunch is especially nice, with offerings like the chestnut pancakes or the wild mushroom and truffle cheese scramble. The highlight of it all is dining on the patio and people watching while enjoying your glass of wine. Volterra also has a private drawing room for up to 85 guests, adorned with Swarovski chandeliers and a Dale Chihuly drawing wall. Allow extra time for parking in this busy neighborhood.

The Walrus and the Carpenter, 4743 Ballard Ave. Northwest, Seattle, WA 98107; (206) 395-9227; Ballard; www.thewalrusbar .com; $. A stroll to the back of historical Ballard's Kolstrand Building reveals a milky white oyster bar gleaming with natural light. Here you will find 4 to 10 types of oysters available a day and plenty of other seafood options like steamed clams, mussels, and fried oysters. They also offer charcuterie and other tasty bites. Open 7 days a week from 4 p.m.; take advantage of the bright patio on hot summer days. Chef Renee Erickson of the **Boat Street Cafe** (see p. 64) and business partners Jeremy Price and Chad Dale opened this spot so that people could have a warm, relaxing place to grab a dinner that focuses on local and sustainable seafood at the end of the day.

Landmark Eateries

Carmelita, 7314 Greenwood Ave. North, Seattle, WA 98103; (206) 706-7703; Phinney Ridge; www.carmelita.net; $$. Carmelita may be a vegetarian restaurant but you won't miss the meat. It's not the point here; it's not about creating dishes that taste like beef but all about showcasing seasonal vegetables in all their glory. Since 1996, this restaurant has been a downright neighborly spot with warm hues and a beautiful heated outside patio as well as the more recently added bar. Check the website before you go to find out what's in season and what will be part of your farm-to-table experience.

Le Gourmand, 425 N.W. Market St., Seattle, WA 98107; (206) 784-3463; Ballard; www.legourmand restaurant.com; $$$$; and **Sambar,** (206) 781-4883; www.sambarseattle.com; $$. This hidden French restaurant in Ballard is the ideal mélange of local and seasonal, adopting this religion way back in the '70s before it became trendy. Co-owner and Chef Bruce Naftaly moved to Seattle to pursue his dream as an opera singer, but fate had other plans, and he ended up working his way up in the restaurant business. Lucky for us, he met co-owner, wife, and Chef Sara Naftaly, and together the harmony of classical French food they create has made Le Gourmand one of the best restaurants in town. White tablecloths, elegant food, and rich sauces make this jewel a beautiful spot for a superb dinner. A la carte is available, but the 7-course chef's special tasting menu for $80 is the way to go. Wine pairings available on request. Inquire about the French cooking classes. For more casual drinks, don't miss Sambar, the attached stylish bar, where quality cocktails, an intimate vibe, and a lovely garden make this place a preferred choice for local night owls.

Ray's Boathouse, Cafe & Catering, 6049 Seaview Ave. Northwest, Seattle, WA 98107; **Ray's Boathouse:** (206) 789-3770; www.rays.com/boathouse; $$$; **Ray's Cafe:** (206) 782-0094; www.rays.com/catering; $$. Just a short drive away from the more lively parts of Ballard is a two-story waterfront restaurant and cafe, with a breathtaking bayside view of the Olympic Mountains over Puget Sound. Since 1973, Ray's has been quintessential Northwest, with a focus on sustainable, local seafood. Ray's was the first to re-introduce Olympia oysters, the region's only native oyster, as well as Loughborough Inlet spot prawns and Copper River salmon. After surviving two fires, this casual cafe, upscale restaurant, and catering venue remains a place of many memories for local fish aficionados. My choice here is the cafe on a beautiful day; if you are lucky enough to score a seat on the outdoor deck (call and see if it is open), go for the Penn Cove mussels with Thai red curry and coconut-milk broth, or the tamarind-marinated seared ahi tuna. Check the menu for daily happy hours, when those very same items and many more are almost half the price.

Central

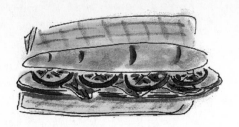

Seattle's core offers so many thrills for food lovers that I couldn't possibly capture them all in one chapter. Not only is this city bursting at the seams with new restaurants opening all the time, but it also has dozens of neighborhoods, each with its own personality and its own walk and talk.

To make sure you don't miss a delicious stop, I've divided the center of Seattle into two chapters, Central and Downtown. In this chapter, you will find Capitol Hill, Central District, Eastlake, First Hill, Madison Park, Madison Valley, Madrona, Magnolia, Queen Anne, South Lake Union, and Westlake. All of these neighborhoods are fairly close to each other, just a quick drive apart.

Not only do these eating establishments affect a neighborhood's personality, but the neighborhoods rub off onto the bakeries, restaurants, and ice-cream parlors. A cupcake shop in Capitol Hill attracts a young, hip crowd while the same cupcake shop elsewhere will be full of polished women with name-brand purses pushing babies in strollers. Capitol Hill boasts a youthful, stylish, open-minded community with a busy nightlife, music, and pop scene, not to mention funky students reading their textbooks in bars. Queen Anne has everything, from a bustling farmers' market sandwiched between eateries and specialty stores to the Space Needle and Seattle Center, part of a busier, urban area. On First Hill, known locally as "Pill Hill," you'll see nurses in blue scrubs dining on their lunch break. In residential Madison Valley, you'll discover Rover's, a five-star restaurant that started its life as a modest bungalow.

In this chapter, you'll also find several of the best restaurants in town, an urban market shopping experience, and places to get the most talked-about bakery goods.

Made Here

Bella Dolce Bakery & Cafe, 2711 E. Madison St., Seattle, WA 98112; (206) 325-9539; Madison Valley. Known for the famous red velvet cake, which comes whole or in cupcake form, this petite bakery is where you can find cookies, house-made granola, brownies, and bread pudding (which might as well be named cake pudding, since it is made of cake instead of bread). The apricot-ginger-pecan scones are a tasty morning treat, and since they are not too sweet and made with whole oats, you can get away with calling them healthy, can't you? They also have sandwiches and lunch items.

Bluebird Homemade Ice Cream & Tea Room, 1205 E. Pike St., Suite 1A, Seattle, WA; (206) 588-1079; Capitol Hill; http://bluebirdseattle.blogspot.com. People watching in Capitol Hill is way better with an ice-cream cone in hand. This laid-back cafe is made up of second-hand couches and wooden tables, the walls decorated with local art. The passed-down furniture is part of the philosophy, a neighborhood cafe with contributions from the community, the kind of place that you feel could actually be part of your home. Bluebird ice cream is made of all-natural dairy products coming from local Washington and Oregon cows with seasonal flavors changing all the time. Find flavors like Stumptown Coffee, Elysian Stout (made with Dragon's Tooth Stout from Elysian Brewing Company), bourbon white chocolate, and Theo Chocolate Chunk. You can also find a nice selection of teas and sandwiches. If you have old books, bring them in and trade in their book exchange library.

Crazy Cherry, 131 Broadway Ave East, Seattle, WA 98102; (206) 324-2550; Capitol Hill. Are you part of the frozen yogurt craze? Not too long ago it seemed that frozen yogurt chains were popping up everywhere, so despite the name which sounds like some big chain, this frozen dessert shop is locally owned. They have smooth and tangy frozen yogurt in flavors like plain, strawberry, and green tea as well as seasonal flavors and toppings such as fresh fruit, mochi, yogurt chips, and nostalgic cereal flavors.

Cupcake Royale and Vérité Coffee, 1111 E. Pike St., Seattle, WA 98122; (206) 328-6544; Capitol Hill; www.cupcakeroyale.com.

(See website for additional locations.) What's not to love about a cupcake cafe that employs the slogan "Legalize Frostitution"? These cupcakes are made with at least 66 percent local ingredients; flour from Shepherd's Grain, fruit from local farmers, and milk and butter from Medowsweet Dairy. The flavors evolve seasonally: in the summer you may find Skagit Valley Strawberry 66, featuring the Skagit farms' summer strawberries, and in February, Death by Chocolate, named Seattle's most lovingly lethal cupcake, featuring Theo Chocolate and Stumptown espresso ganache. Frosting shots are available for those who prefer the frosting without the cake. And because cupcakes taste better with coffee, Vérité Coffee is located in the same spot, serving up the popular Stumptown coffee.

Dilettante on Broadway, 538 Broadway Ave. East, Seattle, WA 98102; (206) 329-6463; Capitol Hill; www.dilettante.com. (See website for additional locations.) When long, stressful days at work call for chocolate and cocktails, pull up a chair at this chocolate martini bar. With multiple locations across Seattle, the Capitol Hill location is home to a chocolate cafe with dim lighting and a quiet atmosphere, and a martini bar area with savory snacks, a Hungarian-Austrian-inspired menu, and happy hour every day from 5 to 7 p.m., with half off all chocolate martinis. Recommended: Ephemere dark- or milk-chocolate truffles, or try a slice of the four-layer mocha praline torte. Other locations have a quick cafe feel and though they have no martini bar, they will definitely fill your chocolate needs.

Eltana, 1538 12th Ave., Seattle, WA, 98122; (206) 724-0660; Capitol Hill; www.eltana.com; $. Sometimes all it takes is a good bagel and a smear. Capitol Hill's Eltana is a bagel haven with natural light shining through the shop. These bagels are boiled in honeyed water for a touch of sweetness then baked in a wood-fired oven. They are rolled by hand and seeded on both sides. But it doesn't end here. The spreads, well they are the cream of the crop. There are choices like Date Walnut Cream Cheese, Eggplant Pomegranate Spread, and Fava Bean Mint Spread. The cafe is family-friendly and a great place to read a book with your breakfast.

The Essential Baking Company, 2719 E. Madison St., Seattle, WA 98112; (206) 328-0078; Madison Valley; www.essentialbaking .com. For a full description see the North listing, p. 5.

Grand Central Bakery, 1616 Eastlake Ave. East, Seattle, WA 98102; (206) 957-9505 or (206) 957-9508; Eastlake; www.grand centralbakery.com. For a full description see the Downtown listing, p. 101.

Le Fournil, 3230 Eastlake Ave. East, Seattle, WA 98102; (206) 328-6523; Eastlake; www.le-fournil.com. Open since 1997, this classic French bakery and cafe has a large selection of intricate tarts, quiches, croissants, cookies, and baked goods. The crusty baguettes are a star with local restaurants—including the whimsical **Nettletown** (see p. 77), a quick drive down the street—which use them to make amazing sandwiches. The daily lunch special includes an entree, dessert, and drink for $8.99. They have a parking area in the back so you can save your money for the goodies.

Le Reve Bakery & Cafe, 1805 Queen Anne Ave. North, Suite 100, Seattle, WA 98109; (206) 623-REVE (7383); Queen Anne; http://lerevebakery.com. This dreamy French bakery on Queen Anne has become a hangout for morning coffees and pastries. Here you will find French macarons, croissants, Danishes, tarts, and cakes freshly baked throughout the day, as well as sandwiches, a nice selection of salads, and hot soups. They serve coffee from local Olympia Coffee Roasting Company. Recommended: the twice-baked almond croissant and *pain au chocolat* with chocolate in every bite.

Louisa's Cafe & Bakery, 2379 Eastlake Ave. East, Seattle, WA 98102; (206) 325-0081; Eastlake; www.louisascafe .com. This cafe and bakery has baked goods of gargantuan proportions—oatmeal cookies, peanut butter cookies, cinnamon rolls—bread rolls the size of salad plates, huge bagels, and other guilty pleasures. They also have sandwiches and a full menu for breakfast, lunch, and dinner. The old-school atmosphere and wooden tables and chairs make it a great option for book club meetings or small groups. They are open Mon through Sat for breakfast, lunch, and dinner and Sun for brunch only.

Macrina Bakery, 615 W. McGraw St., Seattle, WA 98119; (206) 283-5900; Queen Anne; www.macrinabakery.com. For a full description see the Downtown listing, p. 103. This is a smaller and cozier location.

Madison Park Bakery, 4214 E. Madison St., Seattle, WA 98112; Madison Park; (206) 322-3238; Madison Park; www.madisonpark bakery.com. This little old-fashioned bakery is where you can find mini two-bite cinnamon or pecan rolls known as cinnamon cups along with lots of cookies, doughnuts, and savory items like ham and cheese croissants (the Lemon Bars are highly recommended). Get your treat and then stroll around the beautiful neighborhood. They also bake fresh bread daily and they do special orders for cakes and wedding cakes.

Molly Moon's Homemade Ice Cream, 917 E. Pine St., Seattle, WA 98122; (206) 708-7947; Capitol Hill; www.mollymoonicecream .com. For a full description see the North listing, p. 10.

Nielsen's Pastries, 520 2nd Ave. West, Seattle, WA 98119; (206) 282-3004; Queen Anne; www.nielsenspastries.com. Nobody expects a sweet, homey bakery in the middle of busy lower Queen Anne, but Nielsen's Pastries is a landmark Danish pastry shop. Open since 1965 (though it started in another location) this bakery and cafe is where you get *kringles,* huge, layered, buttery, pretzel-shaped Danish pastries with an almond-and-custard filling large enough for six people. Individual apple *kringles* are available, along with *snitters* (a flat cinnamon roll with custard icing), and the most talked-about Potato—no actual potato here, but puffed pastry filled with custard and marzipan and rolled in cocoa powder that resembles a spud. Come around at happy hour every day from 2:30 to 3:30 p.m., when you get a free pastry with the purchase of a Zoka espresso, and sit back in the cozy old-fashioned seating area with that book you have been meaning to finish.

North Hill Bakery, 518 15th Ave. East, Seattle, WA 98112; (206) 325-9007; Capitol Hill; www.northhillbakery.com. This is a small, intimate neighborhood bakery with checkerboard floors and a few chairs. They specialize in cakes, with varieties like coconut, chocolate, lemon chiffon, and carrot, just to name a few. The fresh pastries are made daily and include croissants (even vanilla ones), savory biscuits, brioches, cinnamon rolls, *pain au chocolat,* cookies, and coffee cakes. One of the unexpected finds is a little round oat cake, a biscuit that is not particularly sweet, which can be eaten alone or topped with a savory or sweet topping.

Oh! Chocolate, 3131 East Madison St., Suite 100, Seattle, WA 98112; (206) 329-8777; Madison Park; www.ohchocolate.com. (See website for additional locations.) These lovely chocolate shops are where you find handmade chocolates in small batches, rich creamy truffles and chews made of roasted and toasted coconut and nuts, and many other chocolate favorites. You will be charmed by the quality of their chocolates as well as the inviting personalities of those who work in the store. Sign up for one of their chocolate classes where you can temper, dip, and learn to your chocolaty heart's content.

Old School Frozen Custard, 1316 E. Pike, Seattle, WA 98122; (206) 324-2586; Capitol Hill; www.oldschoolfrozen custard.com. Frozen dessert lovers can find comfort in this silky, creamy dessert made fresh every 2 to 3 hours. Vanilla and chocolate can be found here daily, and the third flavor rotates; check the mega calendar on the website for an update on the flavors. Check the blackboard in the store for signature Sunday combinations with aliases like the Cheerleader, made of 2 scoops of vanilla, strawberry, and white chocolate, or the Truffle, 2 scoops of vanilla, caramels, pecans, and hot fudge.

Piroshki on Madison, 1219 Madison St., Seattle, WA 98104; (206) 624-1295; First Hill; and **Piroshki on 3rd,** 710 3rd Ave.,

Seattle, WA 98104; (206) 322-2820; Downtown; www.piroshkires
taurant.com. Piroshkis are Russian turnovers loaded with fillings,
a convenient and cheap (under $5) carb-loaded snack for cold
winter days when you are craving something on the go. Preference
depends on your mood, but it goes without saying that anything
with potatoes and cheese will hit the spot. The dough is soft and
not greasy, with fillings like potato and cabbage, spinach, eggs,
cheese, mushrooms, rice—and the list goes on. They also have a
selection of sweet desserts including fresh fruit pies, shortbread
cookies, and poppy-seed rolls.

Sugar Bakery & Cafe, 1014 Madison St., Seattle, WA 98104;
(206) 749-4105; First Hill; www.sugarbakerycafe.com. Decorated
with pink walls and hanging rolling pins, Stephanie Crocker's adorable bakery really knows how to make sweet treats—cookies of all
types, including chocolate cookies and lemon crunch cookies, and
over-the-top cupcakes like sticky-bun cupcakes. In the morning,
salted caramel croissants fly out the door so quickly that only the
early birds take the cake. This bakery with limited seating is really
about eating baked goods made by people who are passionate about
what they do.

Thanh Son Tofu, 118 12th Ave., Seattle, WA 98122; (206) 320-
1316; First Hill. Do you know the feeling of hot tofu in your hands?
I didn't know it until I found this place. This unassuming mini Asian
specialty store sells noodles and other basic food products, along
with containers of house-made tofu in all different flavors. When

Happy Hours!

When you are aching for some restaurant food but really can't afford the prices, happy hour saves the day. Timing your afternoon snack or your late night bites can get you a taste of what a restaurant is about at a fraction of the price. A large number of local restaurants offer food items for their daily happy hours to go with the budget-happy drink prices, check the websites before you leave the house. Do note that happy hours may change periodically and in many cases are not available on weekends. Here are just a few favorites in the pond of happy hour goodness.

The happy hour at **Toulouse Petite** (see p. 83) is one of a kind. They offer 75 happy hour food items, many priced less than $5, in addition to drink specials (daily 4 to 5:30 p.m. and 10 p.m. to 1 a.m.).

It sounds almost too good to be true, but during happy hour at **Serious Pie** (see p. 132) the mini pizza pie combinations are available for $5 a pie (Mon through Fri 3 to 5 p.m.)!

For a truly unique and casual dining experience, try the early and late night happy hours at the bar at **Poppy** (see p. 79). The early

you get to the counter, you can ask for the plain tofu and a large chunk of hot tofu made just before you got there will magically land between your fingers. You will never touch store-bought tofu again, and to add to the magic, it is dirt cheap. Be sure to bring cash since they don't take credit cards. Checks are accepted.

session will get you thalis for $5 while late night offers $6 naanwiches (Sun through Thurs 5 to 7 p.m. and 9 to 10 p.m.).

Been hankering for some beef at the **Metropolitan Grill** (see p. 144) but can't afford the price tag? Swing by the happy hour and find items like "The Works Burger" or "Smoky Buffalo Wings" for $6 and under (Mon through Fri 3 to 6 p.m.).

For oysters, check out **Anchovies & Olives** (see p. 63) oyster power hour for a $1 each (Sun through Thurs 5 to 6 p.m. and 10 p.m. to close) or **Elliot's Oyster House's** (see p. 140) progressive oyster happy hour (Mon through Fri 3 to 6 p.m.).

Some more happy hours: **Spring Hill** (see p. 174) (Tues through Fri 5:45 to 7 p.m.); **Bastille** (see p. 21) (daily 4:30 to 6 p.m. and Sun through Thurs 10 p.m. to midnight); **Palace Kitchen** (see p. 145) (Mon through Fri 4:30 to 6 p.m.); and **Dinette** (see p. 67) (Tues through Sat 5 to 6:30 p.m. and Fri through Sat 9 to 11 p.m.).

Some happy hours may change hours with the seasons so check the websites before you go.

Top Pot Doughnuts, 325 W. Galer, Seattle, WA 98119; (206) 631-2120; Queen Anne; www.toppotdoughnuts.com. (See website for additional locations.) For a full description see the Downtown listing, p. 108.

Wink Cupcakes, 1817 Queen Anne Ave. North, Seattle, WA 98109; (206) 856-1600; Queen Anne; www.winkcupcakes.com. In the Queen Anne Neighborhood, this lovable little cupcake shop has some beautifully decorated cupcakes in large or small sizes with flavors like vanilla bean, red velvet, Champagne, Guinness, and more. They also have a rotating list of daily cupcakes to choose from, as well as gluten-free and vegan cupcakes by special order. The seating area is small, but it seems to be a great place for a quick stop. Deliveries available to certain areas around town.

Specialty Stores & Markets

A & J Meats & Seafood, 2401 Queen Anne Ave. North, Seattle, WA 98109; (206) 284-3885; Queen Anne. A & J Meats & Seafood is an old-fashioned butcher shop with top-quality meat, from house-made sausages to lamb shanks, lamb shoulder steaks, pork chops, beef, veal, and more. All the steaks and roasts are aged a minimum of 30 days. In addition to the highest quality meats, the customer service is excellent; the staff is willing to help with suggestions or your questions. In the same space, you will find **Wild Salmon Seafood Market** (see p. 63) and **McCarthy & Schiering Wine Merchants**.

Bar Ferd'nand, 1531 Melrose Ave., Seattle, WA 98122; (206) 623-5882; Capitol Hill; www.ferdinandthebar.com. Bar Ferd'nand is a modern wine bar and shop with beers and wines by the glass and a vast selection of wines by the bottle for you to take home for your next dinner party or evening at home. They have snacks like olives, oysters, cheese plates, and pequillo pepper with salted fish.

Bill the Butcher, 2911 E. Madison St., Seattle, WA 98112; (206) 402-5079; www.billthebutcher.com. (See website for additional locations.) This butcher shop looks more like a specialty food shop than your old-school butcher. It's a great place to find items like marbled steaks, natural pork, homemade sausage, charcuterie, and wild game. The staff is attentive and helpful, ready to answer any questions you might have. They also sell gourmet cheeses, crackers, and condiments.

CakeSpy Shop, 415 E. Pine St., Seattle, WA 98122; (206) 325-1592; Capitol Hill; http://cakespyshop.com. CakeSpy blogger Jessie Oleson opened this compact two-story shop so she could showcase her original artwork and promote the creations of local artists. This shop has a huge assortment of trinkets and knickknacks, many are food-related but not all. You will find CakeSpy's own mugs decorated with animated cupcakes, French toast stamps, oven mitts, aprons, cupcake molds, and other fun gifts for food lovers. Recommended: Look for CakeSpy's illustrated cards and prints with the celebrity cupcake known as Cuppie. Orders can be made online.

The Cheese Cellar, 100 4th Ave. North, Suite 150, Seattle, WA 98109; (206) 404-2743; Queen Anne; www.thecheesecellar.com. Oh, how I love finding cheese in unexpected places. Hidden just a hop, skip, and jump from the Space Needle is a humble cheese shop that carries a large selection of artisanal cheeses from England, Italy, Spain, France, and local farms. The cheese is cut to order, and the store carries all the other goodies that complement the cheese—wine, crackers, and more. The friendly owners, Dennis and Theresa, will customize your cheese plate and gifts, or just call and join the cheese of the month club, and every month a fresh trio of cheeses will land on your doorstep.

Chef Shop, 1425 Elliott Ave. West, Seattle, WA 98119; (206) 286-9988; Interbay; www.chefshop.com. This online food lover's oasis is based out of Seattle. Chef Shop has imported products from fresh pasta to specialty cocoa. They have a large selection of vinegars, oils, spices, hard-to-find food ingredients, and kitchen staples, and the friendly and knowledgeable owners, Eliza Ward and Tim Mar, can help with all your choices. If you are ready to delve into the world of higher quality balsamics, honeys, or oils, they will lead you through a tasting. Fun find: fennel pollen, which is an intense aromatic version of fennel that could be used as seasoning in just about anything and it works well with chicken or fish. When you are done shopping here, stop by **Mustapha's Fine Foods of**

Morocco (see p. 60), just two doors away. They ship to anywhere in the US and all over the world as well.

Chocolopolis, 1527 Queen Anne Ave. North, Seattle, WA 98109; (206) 282-0776; Queen Anne; www.chocolopolis.com. This intimate chocolate shop is organized much like a wine store, with chocolate bars arranged by the geographic origin of the cacao bean. Owner Lauren Adler is adamant about sharing her knowledge in the field and goes about this by carrying all the finest in the chocolate department, educating through chocolate classes and in-store events, and allowing people to sample and compare. Chocolate happy hours take place every Thursday from 5 to 9 p.m. and focus mostly on bean-to-bar chocolate with lots of samples and explanations. Limited seating is available. Recommended: Chocolopolis spicy drinking chocolate or a Chocolopolis Madagascar or Colombia single-origin truffle made by the Chocolopolis chocolatier.

Eat Local, 2400 Queen Anne Ave. North, Seattle, WA 98109; (206) 328-3663; Queen Anne; www.eatlocalonline.com. (See website for additional locations.) This Queen Anne shop has a long list of frozen menu items to take home and heat up so that our busy lives don't prevent us from a home-cooked meal. All the food is prepared with Northwest grass-fed meats, free-range chicken, and organic or sustainably grown produce. They also sell prepared rabbit or elk entrees, artisan crackers, granola, and specialty products. The store also carries many local brands, such as Empire Ice Cream, Theo Chocolate, Fish Tale Organic Beer, and Parker Pickles. Insider tip: Look in the discount freezer for discounted products, which might not have made the cut based on appearance; this is where I find fresh pasta at half price.

George's Sausage and Deli on Madison, 907 Madison St., Seattle, WA 98104; (206) 622-1491; First Hill. Since 1983, this Polish delicatessen has been the place to find Polish sausages, dried salami, pork loin, bacon, twice-smoked sausages, and more. All the smoking and butchery is done in the back of the shop. The walls are lined with imported specialty European products such as cookies, chocolates, canned herring, and more. The real deal here is the ever-so-generous and inexpensive meat-filled sandwiches. Build your own, choosing your favorite meats, cheeses, and breads. Lunchtime lines fill the store, but they move quickly. Rye please!

Marigold and Mint, 1531 Melrose Ave., Seattle, WA 98122; (206) 682-3111; Capitol Hill; www.marigoldandmint.com. This Parisian-style flower shop has flowers for any occasion, but what surprises is everything else that encourages you to wake up and smell the roses. They have vintage gifts, soaps, aprons, and even seasonal produce. Here you can pick up some last-minute embellishments for a dinner party or just look for some gifts to spoil yourself.

Melrose Market, 1501–1535 Melrose Ave., Seattle, WA 98122; Capitol Hill; www.melrosemarketseattle.com. Capitol Hill is home to

Melrose Market, a precious jewel of an indoor market boasting large windows, roomy architecture, and an atmosphere that makes you feel like you've entered a dreamy farmhouse. This market is a one-stop haven for food lovers and people who like to entertain. Here you can also find a music store and other shops, including **Calf and the Kid, Sitka & Spruce** (see p. 81), **Bar Ferd'nand** (see p. 54), and **Rain Shadow Meats** (see p. 61).

Metropolitan Market, 100 Mercer St., Seattle, WA 98109; (206) 213-0778; Queen Anne; www.metropolitan-market.com. (See website for additional locations.) Since 1971 food lovers have been shopping at this locally owned, stylish supermarket that blends the basic groceries with hard-to-find, local products. *Cosmopolitan* magazine cited the Queen Anne location as the best place to land a date (in the produce section), but as far as food goes, they have everything that one needs to cook a perfect meal at home: rich produce, a plentiful cheese section, fresh breads, cakes, condiments, and more. The special touches—local products, specialty cheeses, charcuterie, knowledgeable staff, an eclectic selection of wine, free-range rotisserie chicken, the sweetest peaches in town, and quality prepared foods—make this place a local go-to market for food aficionados. Fun tidbit: The late Julia Child was a regular customer, and when in town, she would buy fresh Alaskan salmon and have it shipped to the United Kingdom.

Mustapha's Fine Foods of Morocco, 1417 Elliot Ave. West, Seattle, WA 98119; (206) 382-1706; Interbay; www.mustaphas .com. One word: harissa. That's all I have to say.

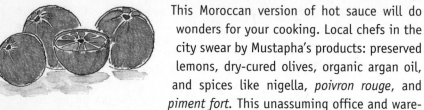 This Moroccan version of hot sauce will do wonders for your cooking. Local chefs in the city swear by Mustapha's products: preserved lemons, dry-cured olives, organic argan oil, and spices like nigella, *poivron rouge,* and *piment fort.* This unassuming office and warehouse is where you can purchase these products. If you can't make it to this location, you can find these products at the top specialty stores in town. When you are done, go to **Chef Shop** (see p. 56) two doors down for additional ingredients to prepare a feast. Recommended: a jar of the M'hamsa Couscous or the *poivron rouge,* made of *niora,* a small round pepper found in Morroco. Don't leave without the harissa; it adds a spicy kick to any sandwich or sauce. See Mustapha Haddouch's recipe for **Sashimi Salmon with Argan Oil** on p. 202.

Pasta & Co, 1935 Queen Anne Ave. North, Seattle, WA; 98109; (206) 283-1182; Queen Anne; www.pastaco.com. (See website for additional locations.) This specialty, gourmet, and take-out shop has everything one needs for an enjoyable meal at home. In addition to fresh pasta, they have seasonal entrees such as apricot-Dijon-glazed pork tenderloin, lamb stew de Provence, and chicken potpie, along with lots of specialty ingredients. This home-cooked food can be enjoyed for takeout as well as eating in at Pasta &

Co. This shop is owned by Kurt Beecher Dammeier, the founder of Beecher's, and all the food at this place reflects his philosophy of providing pure food to his customers, with natural, wholesome ingredients that are additive-free and flavorful—a great concept for a busy family or for a quick stop on your way to a picnic. You will also find a large selection of cheeses including Beecher's award-winning cheeses, meats, fresh artisanal breads, and unique condiments to create a healthy and tasty dinner at home. See Kurt Beecher Dammeier's recipe for **Golden Beet Risotto** (made with Beecher's cheese) on p. 205.

Rain Shadow Meats, 1531 Melrose Ave., Seattle, WA 98122; (206) 467-MEAT (6328); Capitol Hill; www.rainshadowmeats.com. Rain Shadow is about connecting with your food—it's a full-service butcher featuring local and sustainable meats, charcuterie, and a custom curing room with knowledgeable staff ready to share their wealth of information. You will find hangar steaks, confit pork belly, confit duck gizzards, homemade sausages, and various cuts of meat. Do you want a whole pig or whole animal? They can do it. This is old-school butchery in a modern atmosphere.

Seattle Caviar Company, 2922 Eastlake Ave. East, Seattle, WA 98102; (206) 323-3005; Eastlake; www.caviar.com. Since 1990 Dale and Betsy Sherrow have been sharing their passion for caviar in this specialty store that carries a large variety of caviar, including sustainable options, as well as caviar accompaniments and other delicacies like *foie gras,* truffles, and gourmet condiments. Perhaps the most important thing to know about this place is that you will feel welcome and comfortable asking questions and exploring; with $10 tastings offering you the chance to try about 6 different caviars. French Champagne is offered for purchase by the glass as well. If you decide to pick up some caviar, the tasting fee will go toward the purchase. Overnight deliveries are offered via FedEx to all parts of the United States.

Trader Joe's, 112 W. Galer St., Seattle, WA 98119; (206) 378-5536; Queen Anne; www.traderjoes.com. (See website for additional locations.) This specialty grocery chain will make you feel like you are lost in the Caribbean with staff in Hawaiian shirts. You will hear bells shaking but that is just the way the staff communicate around this store. No pirates around, but you will find healthy food products without artificial colors, additives, and MSG at competitive prices. This store is small and intimate, yet clean and organized. Indulge in their healthy snacks, staples, breads, produce, and a wide range of ready-made foods to take home, including salads and sandwiches. The best things to get here are cheeses at low prices and affordable wines.

Whole Foods Market, 2210 Westlake Ave., Seattle, WA 98121; (206) 621-9700; Westlake; www.wholefoodsmarket.com. (See website for additional locations.) With five locations across Seattle and its surrounding areas, Whole Foods Market, founded in Austin, Texas, in 1980, continues to be an eclectic supermarket offering high-quality natural and organic products, a wide range of produce, a spacious bulk section, fresh bakery items, house-made items, and one of the best salad bars around. In the Puget Sound–area stores, you'll find a wide range of products grown and produced locally in Washington, Oregon, and British Columbia. Look for items under the Whole Food private label names of 365 Everyday Value or 365 Organic Everyday Value for quality products at an affordable price.

Wild Salmon Seafood Market, 2401 Queen Anne Ave. North, Seattle, WA 98109; (206) 217-FISH (3474); Queen Anne; www.wildsalmonseafood .com. (See website for additional locations.) The Queen Anne location of this fish market is located right between **A & J Meats & Seafood** (see p. 54) and **McCarthy & Schiering Wine Merchants.** They have a large selection of high-quality seafood including oysters, crab, lobster, shrimp, clams, mussels, and smoked salmon. The emphasis is on fresh product and the service is friendly, and the staff is knowledgeable.

Food Lovers' Faves

Anchovies & Olives, 1550 15th Ave., Seattle, WA 98122; (206) 838-8080; Capitol Hill; www.ethanstowellrestaurants.com/anchovies andolives; $$. Focus is a great asset in the restaurant business. So when cravings for seafood arise, here's where you can take them. With its large windows, banquet seating around the walls, a small patio for summer evenings, and a light wooden bar, this Italian-inspired restaurant from the Ethan Stowell Restaurants group is where items like handmade tagliatelli and smoked tuna unite, or black cod is married with ingredients like escarole, fingerling potatoes, and goat horn chili peppers. Get there for oyster power hour—$1 oysters, $2 beers, and $5 glasses of Prosecco—Sun through Thurs, 5 to 6 p.m., and 10 p.m. to closing. Here you'll find geoduck, mussels, and what it takes to be named a Best New Restaurant by *Bon Appétit*. See Chef Ethan Stowell's recipe for **Gnocchetti with Pancetta, Spring Onions & English Peas** on p. 196.

Boat Street Cafe & Kitchen, 3131 Western Ave., Seattle, WA 98121; (206) 632-4602; Queen Anne; www.boatstreetcafe.com; $$. Hidden in Queen Anne amongst a plethora of office lofts (follow the ramp to the bottom) is the famous Boat Street Cafe & Kitchen. Known for its Provençal flair and its local ingredients, this elegant restaurant will make you feel far from the city while enjoying the simplicity of a country-style retreat. Entrees may include items like Boat Street crab cakes with hot banana pepper confit and pickled peppers, or house-made fennel and red-wine sausage. Try the renowned Boat Street Pickles and the Amaretto bread pudding with a rum-butter cream sauce. Chef Renee Erickson is the chef of Boat Street Cafe, and Susan Kaplan is the chef of Boat Street Kitchen, holding lunch, brunch, and private events.

The Book Bindery, 198 Nickerson St., Seattle, WA 98109; (206) 283-2665; Queen Anne; www.bookbinderyrestaurant.com; $$$. Located in the most magical spot in Queen Anne, 2 blocks from the Fremont Bridge, is the Book Bindery, a restaurant of quiet yet approachable elegance with soft lighting and a breathtaking view. Attached to the **Almquist Family Vintners** cellars, this restaurant was once an old book bindery. The menu is local and seasonal, and you might find items like sweetbreads with caramel-apple puree and wild arugula, or *hamachi crudo*. The *foie gras* terrine is a popular favorite. For smaller bites, order off the rotating bar menu with snacks like truffle fries.

Cafe Presse, 1117 12th Ave., Seattle, WA 98122; (206) 709-7674; Capitol Hill; www.cafepresseseattle.com; $$. From the owners of **Le Pichet** (see p. 128) comes a more laid-back French cafe, otherwise known as Presse by the locals. Your choice of magazines and newspapers to read adorn the entrance, and the ambience, as lovely as the food, changes throughout the day. Mornings feel like a beautiful cafe, students nibbling on eggs and toast; evenings transform into a bistro feel where diners enjoy a nice selection of inexpensive wines by the glass with dinner. The comfortable bar in front of the window overlooks the patio, where casual tables and the laid-back vibe make it the ideal place to break open a copy of the *New York Times*. The menu has items like charcuterie, a selection of egg plates, salads, roasted chicken, sandwiches, and other French-inspired classics. Presse opens at 7 p.m. and closes at 2 a.m. Recommended: croque madame and steak frites.

Cicchetti, 121 E. Boston St., Seattle, WA 98102; (206) 859-4155; Eastlake; http://serafinaseattle.com/cicchetti; $$. The name Cicchetti (pronounced chi-KET-tee) indicates small plates of food; in this case Mediterranean flavors and creative cocktails make this bar and restaurant a lively place for a night out with some friends. The menu rotates frequently, but you might find items along the lines of Moroccan lamb-sausage pizza with tomato-pomegranate sauce or root vegetable tagine with dates and couscous. This is one of the places that actually has happy hours on Saturday, so check the website for more information. Cicchetti is located behind **Serafina** (see p. 91), a classic Italian restaurant from the same owner, Susan Kaufman. Free parking for customers is available in the Leavengood Architects building on Newton Street.

Crush, 2319 E. Madison St., Seattle, WA 98112; (206) 302-7874; Madison Valley; www.chefjason wilson.com/crush.html; $$$$. Winning Best Chef Northwest 2010 for the James Beard Foundation is a big deal in the restaurant world, and just one of the umpteenth titles that Chef Jason Wilson has earned for Crush, his restaurant located in a petite two-story house. The cuisine is Modern American with classical French technique; the utmost care goes into every detail, from the ingredients sourced from local farmers and purveyors to the service and presentation. You might find braised Painted Hills beef short ribs with Yukon potato puree, bacon, and sage-scented baby carrots, or king salmon slow roasted in a bed of Douglas fir with chanterelles and brown-butter carrot and cauliflower. Here you will find the finest cheese and the highest quality fish, beef, and ingredients from local growers as well as vegetables and herbs from the Crush garden, just blocks from the restaurant. To get the Crush experience, trust the chef by opting for either the 6-course tasting menu or the chef's grand tasting menu.

Dinette, 1514 E. Olive Way, Seattle, WA 98122; (206) 328-2282; Capitol Hill; www.dinetteseattle.com; $$. The days of European salons as meeting places for big thinkers may be extinct, but Dinette's loving atmosphere, with its intricate platters on the wall and antique feel, is just the place for thinkers: a comforting lounge and restaurant with decorated tea cups and assorted plates in busy Capitol Hill. Chef Melissa Nyffeler's long-lost love for sandwiches shows in her fancy variations on toasts. Popular items include their Frittata Toast (thin-sliced omelets tossed with white truffle oil and frisée) and Tuscan-style chicken liver mousse with spicy pickled peppers on toast. For heartier meals, try the smoked pork chop over soupy corona beans with radish, kale, and pickled rhubarb, or the house-made ricotta gnocchi, tomatoes, homemade Italian-style sausage, fresh basil, and Parmesan. Check the website for happy hour information.

CRAVING FAST FOOD?
HEAD TO DICK'S DRIVE-IN

A Seattle icon since 1954, Dick's is where Seattleites go to satisfy their quick burger craving. It's a local institution with fast food to the max with a side of memories and nostalgia. The $2.50 deluxe burger, the $1.40 fries, and the $2 milk shake are some of the reasons Dick's parking lot is filled through the days and late nights. The secret of Dick's success is simple: Why eat at a national fast food chain when you can get cheap and quick food from one that has been close to the hearts of Seattleites for over five decades? Visit www.dicksdrivein.com; multiple locations; $.

Elliot Bay Cafe (located in the Elliot Bay Book Company), 1521 10th Ave., Seattle, WA 98122; (206) 436-8482; Capitol Hill; www .elliottbaycafe.com; $. (See website for additional location [without bookstore].) If you ask me, there is nothing like eating lunch with a good book nestled between your fingers. One of my favorite places for a quick lunch is this cafe owned by Chef Tamara Murphy and located in this spacious independent bookstore, with its homey atmosphere, natural wood floors, and endless shelves of books. The Capitol Hill menu is short but with creative takes on crepes, hearty soups, sandwiches, and salads, all using the best local ingredients. The Pioneer Square location does not have a bookstore, but it does have a larger menu and space for events.

El Mestizo, 526 Broadway, Seattle, WA 98122; (206) 324-2445; First Hill; www.elmestizorestaurant.com; $$. It's all about the authentic Mexican cooking. Everything is fresh and so full of flavor, and the tortillas come out warm and steaming. At dinner, try unique dishes like the *ensalada de nopal,* a salad made of cactus-leaf strips, tomatoes, onions, and fresh herbs; the *alambres,* sliced steak pan-seared with bacon, bell peppers, onions, and melted Oaxaca cheese; or the crowd favorite *enchiladas de mole,* shredded chicken breast and mole sauce rolled in homemade corn tortillas and topped with crumbled *queso blanco* and *crema fresca.* Lunch is a different scene with counter service and tamales, naked burritos, create-your-own burrito, and more. Either way, the food here will leave you plotting your next visit on the way to the car.

Emmer & Rye, 1825 Queen Anne Ave. North, Seattle, WA 98109; (206) 282-0680; Queen Anne; www.emmerandrye.com; $$. Two stories of memories seem to move through the walls of this old but endearing Victorian house, where Chef Seth Caswell, with an emphasis on supporting the community's food purveyors, cooks up local, seasonal farm-to-table food. Open for lunch, brunch, and dinner with items in half-, full-, taste- and appetizer-size portions.

This restaurant, named after two ancient grains, has become a Queen Anne neighborhood hangout for families and foodies alike.

Ezell's Famous Chicken; 501 23rd Ave., Seattle, WA 98122; (206) 324-4141; Capitol Hill; www.ezellschicken.com. (See website for additional locations.) This fast-food joint has reached iconic status with Oprah publicly professing her love, and people lining up for the Southern fried chicken, the fresh rolls, and the fried-up gizzards or livers. There is no seating here, so plan to pick up and go. Their famous fried chicken has kept Seattleites licking their fingers for over 20 years.

The Harvest Vine, 2701 E. Madison, Seattle, WA 98122; (206) 320-9771; Madison Valley; www.har vestvine.com; $$. Commitment-phobes will love this intimate tapas spot that allows you to taste several dishes and encourages conversation around the table. Harvest Vine is Madison Valley's treasured restaurant, where emphasis is on the Spanish Basque region combined with sustainability and the finest Northwest and Spanish ingredients. The extensive Spanish wine list has over 200 bottles. Inquire about the paella dinners on Tuesday nights, or spend your weekend mornings enjoying a Spanish brunch.

Homegrown Sandwiches, 1531 Melrose Ave., Seattle, WA 98122; (206) 682-0935; Capitol Hill; www.eathomegrown.com; $. (See website for additional locations.) High wooden tables perched at the window make this sustainable sandwich shop the spot for a nice lunch with a light-filled, earthy ambience. Local organic ingredients are used in myriad tasty sandwich combinations, like the roasted pork (made with pork loin rubbed with Stumptown coffee and cayenne, pickled red onion, apple butter, mixed greens, and sage aioli) or the crab cake sandwich with Zoe's bacon, avocado, mixed greens, hazelnut romesco, and chimichurri served hot on a toasted sesame roll. Many of the sandwiches weigh in at $8.95 and up, but they come in exceptionally large portions with layers and layers of wholesome ingredients. Recommended: the turkey, bacon, and avocado made from local purveyor Zoe's turkey and bacon with Gouda, avocado, mixed greens, tomato, and aioli served hot on toasted whole grain bread.

How to Cook a Wolf, 2208 Queen Anne Ave. North, Seattle, WA 98109; (206) 838-8090; Queen Anne; www.ethanstowellrestaurants .com/howtocookawolf; $$. Named after M. F. K. Fisher's book *How to Cook a Wolf,* this Queen Anne restaurant from the Ethan Stowell Restaurants group embodies the philosophy of celebrating simple ingredients. This intimate space with an open kitchen, Italian finesse, and a hip neighborhood atmosphere is great for lively conversations. The dishes are all representations of how local ingredients and simple techniques can lead to sophisticated dishes. The menu is short and changes every day with small plates that are perfect for sharing. My favorite is the spaghetti with anchovies and chili, a big salty bowl of comfort. No reservations accepted here, so come right when it opens or take advantage of the late-night dining or, on warm evenings, the outdoor seating. See Chef Ethan Stowell's recipe for **Gnocchetti with Pancetta, Spring Onions & English Peas** on p. 196.

June, 1423 34th Ave., (206) 323-4000; Seattle, WA 98122; Madrona; www.juneseattle.com; $$. The name is short and sweet, like the summer months, and owners and Chefs Vuong and Tricia Loc know how to keep it simple and accentuate the best ingredients at this charming Madrona restaurant. The food is French-American, and you might find menu items like geoduck with hot-and-sour apples and ginger or the grilled côte de boeuf with rösti potato for two. Try the braised lamb neck with hand-cut pasta. The menu offers a selection of choices between bites, apps, or dinner, and the restaurant is open for dinner and weekend brunch.

The Kingfish Cafe, 602 19th Ave. East, Seattle, WA 98112; (206) 320-8757; Capitol Hill; http://thekingfishcafe.com; $$. Seattle chefs love to showcase their takes on comfort food, though down-home Southern food is still hard to come by. The Kingfish Cafe is just the place for this. It is decorated with photos of family members sporting suits and hats from the 1900s and has an upbeat vibe with generous portions. Open for lunch and dinner daily, menu items range from salads with fried chicken, gumbo, juicy sandwiches—and the list goes on. Go for the Simply Griddled

Catfish or Down Home Mac and Cheese and end with the red velvet cake, perhaps the largest serving of this cake in Seattle. They don't take reservations, so arrive at the start of service or be prepared to wait in line.

La Bete, 1802 Bellevue Ave., Seattle, WA 98122; (206) 329-4047; Capitol Hill; www.labeteseattle.com; $$. La Bete, meaning "the Beast" in French, is a fairy tale of restaurant. It has a mysterious beauty, with accents like a tree-trunk-edged bar, intricate windows, and detailed tables in a dim, bistro-like atmosphere. Sitting on the bar will give you a bird's-eye view of the kitchen, a crash-course in culinary school as you watch the chefs plate the Northwest ingredients. Menu items include snacks like fried pork rinds with pickled shallots, Manchego cheese in herbed olive oil, and comforting main items like leg of lamb with baby carrots, turnips, pickled ramps, and harissa. La Bete is also great spot for Sunday brunch.

Lark, 926 12th Ave., Seattle, WA 98122; (206) 323-5275; Capitol Hill; www.larkseattle.com; $$; and **Licorous,** 928 12th Ave., Seattle, WA 98122; (206) 325-6947; Capitol Hill; www.licorous.com; $. In a city where honoring farmers has become second nature, Lark eloquently demonstrates this culture. The extensive seasonal menu—divided into sections like cheese, vegetable and grains, meats and charcuterie—is the ultimate blessing as small plates can be shared, and family-style dining is encouraged. Don't overlook the Bluebird Grains Farm farro, a nutty, slightly chewy grain that melds perfectly with seasonal Northwest ingredients. If a drink and a snack is all you need, go next door to Licorous, the happening sister bar where handcrafted cocktails, small batch infusions, liquors, and savory snacks are served in a swanky yet cozy atmosphere.

La Spiga, 1429 12th Ave., Seattle, WA; 98122; (206) 323-8881; Capitol Hill; www.laspiga.com; $$. Friends are always asking me for suggestions on places to bring a party of 6 to 8 people. La Spiga plays the part. With 6,000 square feet and its clean, contemporary wooden accents, large open space, and lively atmosphere, it makes a nice place for dinner with a group or smaller meetings with friends. The food is reminiscent of the Emilia-Romagna region of northern Italy with hand-made pastas and seasonal ingredients from the Northwest. Gluten-free pasta is available on request.

Luc, 2800 E. Madison, Seattle, WA 98112; (206) 328-6645; Madison Valley; www.thechefinthehat.com/luc; $$. When Thierry Rautureau, aka the Chef in the Hat, since he is always seen sporting a fedora, came up with a wild idea to have all his loyal customers pre-purchase $1,000 gift certificates at a 30 percent added value in his next restaurant venture, people jumped on the bandwagon; the names of all his "Founding Diners" are on the walls. Luc, named after Chef Thierry's father, is a neighborhood bistro right near **Rover's** (see p. 90), with cherrywood accents and a whirlwind of energy that gives you the opportunity to enjoy top-notch food in a casual yet happening atmosphere. The food is polished and layered in flavors. Menu items include options like beef bourguignon stew, homemade grilled lamb sausage, and saffron couscous with fennel confit, lemon, and carrot sauce. Recommended: the beef burger with caramelized onions, tomato jam, arugula, Luc's aioli, and fries. Also try the Soufflé Potato Crisps—a city favorite. See Chef Thierry Rautureau's recipe for **Halibut Ceviche with Mango and Cucumber** on p. 203.

Lunchbox Laboratory, 1253 Thomas St., Seattle, WA 98109; (206) 621-1090; South Lake Union; www.lunchboxlaboratory.com; $$. This roomy burger joint will satisfy hefty appetites. There is a burger here for nights when you have had a little too much to drink or feel like you deserve the biggest, juiciest, goopiest burger you have ever tasted. The choices are endless: choose your burger, choose your sauce, choose your toppings. Did you ask for bacon? Oh no, you didn't. The layers of bacon are generously out of control. It is all about the burger here!

Marjorie, 1412 E. Union St., Seattle, WA 98122; (206) 441-9842; Capitol Hill; www.marjorierestaurant.com; $$. Marjorie is a contradiction. The ambience is both romantic and bustling, the interior is distinctly moody and vibrant, and the menu is warmly familiar and diverse. But somehow, everything seems to work in unison. Locally sourced ingredients take an eclectic world slant with each component of the plate retaining its integrity and flavor in the combination of a perfect dish. You may think you know what you're getting at Marjorie, but everything comes with an element of surprise.

Meskel Ethiopian Restaurant, 2605 E. Cherry St., Seattle, WA 98122; (206) 860-1724; Central District; $$. I have spent ample time quizzing Ethiopian friends on the best Ethiopian food, and Meskel always makes it to the top of the list. Although there are some other really good places in the same area of town, this one has it all with the best atmosphere, service, and food. The roomy garden and intimate patio seating lead you to feel that you are stepping into the house of an Ethiopian friend. The hospitality is genuine, and the generous spices in Ethiopian food take your dining to a different level. Forget what you know about dining with forks, and allow your fingers to pinch your food with the help of the *injera,* a spongy pita-like bread made of the hard-to-find teff flour. The menu presents a wide array of braised meats, lentil purees, and vegetables stewed into glorious spice combinations. Vegetarians and carnivores alike will love the vegetarian platter. They are well known for the *kitfo,* ground beef with spices and spiced butter. Don't miss the Ethiopian spiced tea.

Mistral Kitchen, 2020 Westlake Ave., Seattle, WA 98121; (206) 623-1922; South Lake Union; http://mistral-kitchen.com; $$ for small plates menu (other menus are additional). The thing about Mistral Kitchen is that there is something for everyone. Your dining style is your choice: a snack and wondrous cocktail at the bar, a fabulous but relaxed lunch, dinner, or weekend brunch in the restaurant's commodious "casual side," or a tasting menu at the Chef's Table or in the restaurant's Jewel Box. Chef and owner William Belickis has created his ultimate playground, and in every aspect, his clear and exacting approach comes across—the flavors are bright and balanced, and the award-winning space by Tom Kundig transports diners to a hipper dimension.

Nettletown, 2238 Eastlake Ave. East, Seattle, WA 98102; (206) 588-3607; Eastlake; http://nettletown.com; $. Eastlake's unassuming takeout/restaurant is one of the best secrets around. Owned by Chef Christina Choi, who was the co-founder (with Jeremy Faber) of **Foraged and Found Edibles**—known for providing Seattle restaurants and farmers' markets with the best foraged goods in town—this place is about bringing the best ingredients and flavors together with local, seasonal, organic, and foraged ingredients. Inspired by her Swiss and Chinese background, the menu includes items like delicious Nettletown noodles (egg noodles served on a bed of greens topped with seasoned wild mushrooms, tea egg, scallions, and toasted garlic oil with five-spice Berkshire pork short rib or baked tofu) and the will-make-you-kick-your-heels-with-joy elk-lemongrass meatball sandwich made with mixed herbs that change seasonally (mint, lemon balm, sorrel) and a mayo-chili sauce. Order the huckleberry or fresh ginger apple sparklers to drink. Lunch is counter service, and takeout is available. The best time to come to avoid the hustle is right after lunch. During dinner, there is table service. Check the website for hours and events.

Nishino, 3130 E. Madison St., Seattle, WA 98112; (206) 322-5800; Madison Park; www.nishinorestaurant.com; $$$. Crisp, clean walls and white tablecloths welcome you into this contemporary sushi restaurant. Classy but not stuffy with gracious service, the menu will provide you with many choices from sushi to noodles as well as tempura, teriyaki, and more. It is a favorite among my Japanese friends who are open to a more modern fusion sushi restaurant, where a la carte items will showcase chicken yakitori or spicy garlic chicken. Sitting at the bar and talking to the sushi chef will offer a customized experience with sushi to suit your taste. Reservations recommended for ordering *omakase*—letting the chef decide what to send out.

Oddfellows, 1525 10th Ave; Seattle, WA 98122; (206) 325-0807; Capitol Hill; www.oddfellowscafe.com; $$. Located in the 1908 Oddfellows building, farmhouse tables, benches, vintage light fixtures, and retro accents bring this place to life. There is nothing odd about this place except for the fact that the 2500-square-foot building works just as well at night as it does by day. In the mornings, nibble on homemade biscuits and eggs or brioche French toast; lunch is filled with creative salads and sandwiches; and at night find items like roasted free range chicken with savory bread pudding or the ever-so-popular meatballs with parmesan polenta and pine nuts. You won't want to miss the whoopie pies. The place is as hip as Capitol Hill yet as laid-back as you want it—a great place to catch up on work on your computer or have drinks at night with friends. It is also a place where kids are welcome.

Olivar, 806 E. Roy St., Seattle, WA 98102; (206) 322-0409; Capitol Hill; www.olivarrestaurant.com; $$. Olivar is a quaint Spanish/French bistro located in Capitol Hill's historic Loveless building, circa 1930. The walls are embellished with a Pushkin fairy tale about a swan that turns into a princess, created by artist V. Shkurkin. Olivar still keeps this art glowing, matching it with wooden tables and a romantic atmosphere—an ideal environment to woo a date or even chat with friends after a movie at the Harvard Exit across the street. Chef Philippe Thomelin cooks French and Spanish small plates—generous in size with seasonal, market-inspired dishes. Order the lamb meatballs known as the *albondigas de cordero* and the handmade gnocchi.

Poppy, 622 Broadway East, Seattle, WA 98102; (206) 324-1108; Capitol Hill; www.poppyseattle.com; $$$$. When Jerry Traunfeld, former executive chef of the renowned **Herbfarm** (see p. 109), opened his own more casual venture, the Seattle dining scene received a renaissance in flavor combinations. Food here is served Indian-style on a *thali*, a selection of small dishes in circular bowls that offers many tastes. The combination of the seasonal Northwest and the Indian-style service give you the opportunity to try a mix of different dishes, including premium meat, fish, and vegetables. This brilliant tug-of-war of flavors weighs in at between $22 and $32. A colorful vegetarian *thali* is available as well as a la carte options like poached oysters with sorrel sauce and bacon and the must-have eggplant fries with salt and honey. Don't miss one of the best dessert deals in town, a $15 dessert *thali* for sharing is an assortment of many different bites. It is casual enough so that you can pop in just for the dessert when that craving hits you. Check the website for $5 happy hour *thalis*.

Quinn's, 1001 E. Pike St., Seattle, WA 98122; (206) 325-7711; Capitol Hill; www.quinnspubseattle.com; $$. One no longer needs to succumb to tasteless germy peanuts with their brewski. Besides, when you are trying to look cool and collected at the bar, you wouldn't want to be wiping your fingers on your jeans. That's why Quinn's gastropub, a pub that focuses on high quality food, is a welcoming concept and one of Capitol Hill's hot spots, with 14 beers on tap, a full bar, a comprehensive menu, and items like oxtail, gnocchi, roasted corn, fontina, and crispy marrow, or rabbit sausage with smoked and compressed watermelon and heirloom tomatoes. Bar snacks here reach new levels with options like duck pâté with watermelon chutney and salt cod fritters with remoulade. Reservations are not accepted; the only exception is the big table on the top level for groups of 8 or more, a fun way to feel like you are having a private party. Recommended: 8-ounce Painted Hills beef burger with cheddar, bacon, mayo, and fries.

re:public, 429 Westlake Ave. North, Seattle, WA 98109; (206) 467-5300; South Lake Union; www.republicseattle.com; $$. This South Lake Union restaurant and bar boasts a lively, urban-chic atmosphere. Reminiscent of a large warehouse with brick walls, industrial design, a nice long bar, and tables from high to low, re:public is a great spot for sharing innovative small plates, house-made pastas, and creative farm-to-table bites. Happy hour has a short menu of inexpensive wines by the glass and *bouchées,* French for "bites," everyday from 4 to 6 p.m.

Serious Pie, 401 Westlake Ave. North, Seattle, WA 98108; (206) 436-0050; South Lake Union; http://tomdouglas.com/index.php/restaurants/serious-pie; $$. For a full description see the Downtown listing, p. 132.

Sitka & Spruce, 1531 Melrose Ave. East, Seattle, WA 98122; (206) 324-0662; Capitol Hill; www.sitkaandspruce.com; $$. Sitka & Spruce is charming restaurant owned by Matt Dillon of **The Corson Building** (see p. 158). Sweet single vases, a wood-burning oven, a large open window bursting with natural light, a communal table, and romantic accents make this place ideal for a lunch or dinner. The menu is short and sweet with seasonal items that are executed with the perfect combination of simplicity and flavor. This farm-to-table experience is in large demand; reservations recommended. Evenings are busy so if you decide to drop in, put your name on the waiting list and grab a drink at **Bar Ferd'nand** (see p. 54) next door.

Spinasse, 1531 14th Ave., Seattle, WA 98122; (206) 251-7673; Capitol Hill; www.spinasse.com; $$$. Located in trendy Capitol Hill, Spinasse is a charming restaurant, from its rustic wooden tables and chairs to its classic, homey ambience and focused cuisine. The food highlights the old-world character of classic Piedmont, a region of

Italy that produces handmade pastas and seasonal ingredients that share numerous similarities with the bounty of the Northwest. Chef Jason Stratton, named a 2010 Best New Chef by *Food & Wine* magazine, puts great pride into the food, integrating artisan local meats and produce. For the ultimate experience, steer toward the *menu degustazione* ($95), a tasting menu that gives you the opportunity to try every antipasto, primo, and secondo on the menu, or reserve the chef's counter on Friday or Saturday night for $100 and partake of an 8- to 13-course menu that gives you an exclusive view into the kitchen. Recommended: *Tajarin al Ragu o burro e salvia*, fine hand-cut egg pasta with ragu or butter and sage. See Chef Jason Stratton's recipe for **Apricot Mostarda di Cremona** on p. 194.

Sushi Kappo Tamura, 2968 Eastlake Ave. E., Seattle, WA 98102; (206) 547-0937; Eastlake; www.sushikappotamura.com; $$$. This sushi restaurant hits all the high notes for a sushi night out: a fresh modern decor, complemented by a traditional sushi experience with a focus on first-class local and seasonal ingredients. Local chefs and food lovers know to come for the cuisine of Chef Taichi Kitamura, a sushi virtuoso who first came to Seattle as an exchange student from Japan. He gets to know his customers, engaging and personalizing the sushi experience. For the top-grade sushi experience order *omakese*—meaning you allow Chef Taichi to choose a tasting menu for you.

Tavern Law, 1406 12th Ave., Seattle, WA 98122; (206) 322-9734; Capitol Hill; www.tavernlaw.com. From the owners of **Spur** (see

p. 132), the popular gastropub in Belltown, Tavern Law is a bar with a speakeasy-inspired atmosphere and classy comfort food. With over 40 cocktails on the list, one need not settle; the bartender will happily create a cocktail that fits your style. Menu items are seasonal, but you can find items like Waygu beef brisket, *foie gras* terrine, and fried peppers paired with chèvre and romesco sauce.

Thai Curry Simple 2, 1122 E Madison St., Seattle, WA, 98122; (206) 325-1494; Capitol Hill; www.thaicurrysimple.com. For a full description see the Downtown listing, p. 135.

Toulouse Petite, 601 Queen Anne Ave. North, Seattle, WA 98119; (206) 432-9069; Queen Anne; www.toulousepetit.com; $$. If finding places where locals hang out is any indication of a good restaurant, then finding places where members of the food industry hang out is the ultimate stamp of approval. The second restaurant from the owner of next door's highly popular **Pesos Kitchen & Lounge,** Toulouse, as the locals call it, is a large restaurant and bar serving fare with a melting pot of cuisines influenced from the French Quarter of New Orleans: Creole and New Orleans French along with Parisian and French countryside touches. The notable decor features over 5,000 pounds of hand-applied and colored plaster, custom metalwork fixtures, and lengthy windows. The happy hours are some of the best in town, with a long list of entrees for under $5, including 15 cocktails for $6.95;

breakfast happy hour is every day from 9 to 11 a.m. and has a long list of items for $6 each. Solo diners can feel totally comfortable at the bar, families are welcome, and the lively atmosphere provides a comfortable feel for everyone. Recommended: the Toulouse Beignets and the Jumbo Barbecued Shrimp New Orleans over Creamy Corn Grits.

Tutta Bella, 2200 Westlake Ave., Suite 112, Seattle, WA 98121; (206) 624 4422; www.tuttabellapizza.com; $$. For a full description see the South listing, p. 163.

Via Tribunali, 913 E. Pike St., Seattle, WA 98122; (206) 322-9234; Capitol Hill; www.viatribunali.net; $$. (See website for additional locations.) When you cross the threshold at any of their four locations, you feel like you have been transported to Naples. The pizzerias are filled with beautiful brick walls, traditionally tiled pizza ovens, and the dining room is adorned with dimly lit candles so you can sense that Italian sensuality everywhere. They opened their first pizzeria in 2004 in the hip and happening Capitol Hill neighborhood, as a Verace Pizza Napoletana (VPN) certified pizzeria, they are held to the strict standards for making true Neapolitan pizza. You will find pizzas like the Margherita (pomodoro, fresh mozzarella, grana, and basil) or the *spaccanapoli* (smoked mozzarella, ricotta, olive, grana, basil, and arugula or prosciutto di Parma. The meal would not be complete without the caprese salad made of tomatoes, basil, and fresh mozzarella or *mozzarella di bufala*.

Vios Cafe & Marketplace, 903 19th Ave. East, Seattle, WA 98112; (206) 329-3236; Capitol Hill; www.vioscafe.com/vioscapitol hill.html; $$; and **Vios Cafe at Third Place,** 6504 20th Ave. Northeast, Seattle, WA 98115; (206) 525-5701; Ravenna; www .vioscafe.com/viosravenna.html; $$. Being the mother of an energetic toddler, this is one of my favorite spots on Capitol Hill. It is rare to find a restaurant that has such a welcoming space for toddlers, with toys and games and a kid-size table with authentic Greek food that makes you feel like you are eating at your *yia yia*'s house. It's the fresh ingredients, the fruity olive oil, and the taste of the Mediterranean that defines dishes like chicken souvlaki, hummus, tzatziki, baba ghanoush, and grilled lamb skewers. Open for lunch and dinner with many options for takeout. Family-style feasts are available for parties of 10 or more at under $30 a person.

Volunteer Park Cafe, 1501 17th Ave. East, Seattle, WA 98112; (206) 328-3155; Capitol Hill; www.alwaysfreshgoodness.com; $$. After a stroll through Volunteer Park, nothing hits the spot more than the beloved and bustling Volunteer Park Cafe, with its mismatched chairs, communal table, and welcoming atmosphere. It's the kind of place that makes your eyes smile. The motto is locally sourced ingredients made with love. Grab a coffee and scone or lunch items like the barbecue pulled pork sandwich or the Brie and apple panini. At dinner, enjoy braised short ribs, simply grilled seafood, hearty pastas, and an abundance of seasonal vegetables, many from the garden out back. Oh, and make sure to save room for something sweet; the desserts are lovely. See Volunteer Park Café's recipe for **Brown Butter Bars** on p. 211.

Landmark Eateries

Cafe Flora; 2901 E. Madison St., Seattle, WA 98112; (206) 325-9100; Madison Park; www.cafeflora.com; $$. It all started in 1990 when three long-time friends decided to buy an old Laundromat space and open a restaurant in Madison Park. All being residents of the area, they wanted to establish a place where locals could meet, and the food would be excellent nonmeat dishes from all over the globe that above all would follow the philosophy of local, organic, and sustainable. Named the best vegetarian restaurant in the Pacific Northwest by the *Vegetarian Times,* this creative and ambitious restaurant brings this genre of food to a new level with eclectic vegan and gluten-free items that are flavorful and hearty. A casual and friendly atmosphere, the menu may include items like nectarine and lemon-cucumber salad, stone-fired pizzas, and lavender ratatouille with chickpea polenta. Brunch is a special treat, and dinner's Oaxaca tacos are recommended.

Canlis, 2576 Aurora Ave. North, Seattle, WA 98109; (206) 283-3313; Queen Anne; www.canlis.com; $$$$. Tucked away in Queen Anne, just 3 miles north of downtown, lies the epitome of a landmark restaurant. Opened in 1954 by Peter Canlis, this fine-dining restaurant continues to top all charts and contests, offering exquisite Northwest cuisine and the most breathtaking views of the city. Although the ownership has been passed down to a younger generation of Canlis, it remains strikingly perfect in every way. Canlis is one of the only places in town where you can never be overdressed; food and service dance in unison, whisking you away to an evening without worries, from the little details like the valet parking to the sommelier introducing you to one of the most comprehensive wine lists in town. In 2008, Chef Jason Franey joined the team and has updated the menu to include modern fine-dining tasting menus with sophisticated dishes. Special requests here are accommodated with grace so don't hesitate to call. If the price tag does not fit your budget, Canlis offers snacks and drinks in the lounge area.

Monsoon, 615 19th Ave. East, Seattle, WA 98112; (206) 325-2111; Capitol Hill; and **Monsoon East,** 10245 Main St., Bellevue, WA

Gluten-Free Living in Seattle

Along with being conscious of the producers of their food, many chefs show awareness for food allergies, intolerances, and gluten-free lifestyles. Restaurants now take precautions to avoid cross contamination with gluten by designating gluten-free areas in the kitchen. Diners living a gluten-free lifestyle should let the waitstaff know the extent of their sensitivity so the restaurant can take the right precautions. Here are some favorites where gluten-free options are available.

Wheatless in Seattle (10003 Greenwood Ave. North, Seattle, WA 98133; 206-782-5735; Greenwood; www.wheatlessinseattle .net) is a delightful gluten-free bakery and cafe that has everything from pizza by the slice to pastries, lasagna, French bread, cheesecakes, turnovers—and the list goes on. The menu is ever-changing with foods that are also egg-free, dairy-free, and soy-free. Check the website for bakeries and pizzerias that carry their products. Fremont's **Flying Apron Bakery** (3510 Fremont Ave. North, Seattle, WA 98103; 206-442-1115; Fremont; www.flyingapron.com) is home to vegan, gluten-free, and wheat-free pastries with cinnamon rolls, cookies, maple bars, breads, and more. The bakery also has a homey seating area and cafe.

Many restaurants have recently taken the plunge into the gluten-free world with special options. **Andaluca** (see p. 139, attached to the Mayflower Hotel in the heart of downtown Seattle, showcases an extensive gluten-free menu. In Madison Park, you will find the iconic vegetarian restaurant **Cafe Flora** (see p. 86) with various gluten-free and vegan options to choose from. **Village Sushi** (4741 12th Ave. Northeast, Seattle, WA 98105; 206-985-6870; University District; www.villagesushiseattle.com) provides a gluten-free sushi experience along with gluten-free hot items like teriyaki chicken. **Zaw** (1424 E. Pine St. at 15th, Seattle, WA 98122; 206-325-5528; Capitol Hill; www.zaw.com; see website for additional locations) offers Artisan Bake at Home Pizza that is gluten-free. The pies are made with wholesome ingredients. **Chaco Canyon Organic Cafe** (4757 12th Ave. NE, Seattle, WA 98105; 206-522-6966; University District; www.chacocanyoncafe.com) has a separate part of the kitchen for preparing gluten-free options and many raw-food menu items as well as pastries. **Anthony's Pier 66 and Bell Street Diner** (2201 Alaskan Way, Seattle, WA 98121; 206-448-6688; Belltown/Waterfront; www.anthonys.com; see website for additional locations) has a separate seafood-heavy, gluten-free menu including appetizers, mains, and desserts. **Volterra** (see p. 38) and **La Spiga** (see p. 74) have gluten-free pasta; call ahead to make sure they are serving it that day. **Plum Bistro** (1429 12th Ave., Seattle, WA 98122; 206-838-5333; Capitol Hill; www.plumbistroseattle.com) has a selection of salads and items that are gluten-free. **Ten Mercer** (10 Mercer St., Seattle, WA, 98109; 206-691-3723, Queen Anne; www.tenmercer.com) in lower Queen Anne offers a gluten-free menu with a selection of salads, meats, seafood, and desserts.

98004; (425) 635-1112; Bellevue; www.monsoonrestaurants.com; $$$. The crisp, minimalistic decor and the lightly shaded wooden tables reveal a chic restaurant over a decade old, serving traditional Vietnamese food with a Northwestern flair. Open for lunch and dinner daily as well as dim sum brunch on the weekends. Appetizers stand out with fresh wraps and rolls, and creative small plates like green papaya salad with grilled prawns and caramelized shallots or grilled Monterey squid stuffed with duck meat, basil, and jicama. During lunch or brunch, order the oxtail pho with Wagyu beef brisket and Wagyu eye of round, a flavorful noodle soup simmered for two days with a rich broth and spices like cardamom, clove, and cinnamon.

Rover's, 2808 E. Madison St., Seattle, WA 98112; (206) 325-7442; Madison Valley; www.thechefinthehat.com/rovers; $$$$. This magical restaurant, hidden in a courtyard in Madison Valley, proves that if your heart is in the right place, then only the finest can come out of it. Chef Thierry Rautureau, otherwise known as the fedora-donning Chef in the Hat, conceived of Rover's in August of 1987. Even after all these years, Rover's remains one of the top restaurants in this city, marrying the techniques and grace of French cuisine with the riches of Northwest ingredients. It's the Chef in the Hat's passion that provides a canvas for spectacular food, with flawless presentation and flavors that harmonize. A la carte options are available, but this is not the place to hold back. Opt for a set menu—the $59 bistro menu, or any of the *degustation*, (French for "tasting menu"), such as the $99 5-course menu or the 8-course

Grand Menu Degustation at $135. Vegetarians can be assured that the $85 vegetarian *degustation* menu provides an equally euphoric dining experience. See Chef Thierry Rautureau's recipe for **Halibut Ceviche with Mango and Cucumber** on p. 203.

Serafina, 2043 Eastlake Ave. East, Seattle, WA 98102; (206) 323-0807; Eastlake; www.serafinaseattle.com; $$. After more than 20 years, Eastlake's Serafina remains a romantic neighborhood restaurant for Italian fare with its gorgeous outdoor patio, rustic atmosphere, and the chitter-chatter of diners that blends into the backdrop. Serafina is about presenting local ingredients in the simplest way. The menu boasts classics like *cozze affumicate,* Taylor Shellfish mussels simmered with smoked tomato, harissa, sweet vermouth, leeks, fresh herbs, and garlic, and Melanzane alla Serafina: thinly sliced eggplant rolled with ricotta cheese, fresh basil, and Parmesan, baked in a tomato sauce, and served over *cappellini aglio e olio*. On warm and even slightly chilly evenings, the much-loved heated patio is where you want to be; seating is available on a first-come, first-served basis. Come in early at around 5:45 p.m. and you are more likely to score a table outside. Free parking for restaurant customers is available in the Leavengood Architects building southeast of Serafina on Newton Street.

Downtown

Mounds of red and yellow tomatoes, piles of purple potatoes, friendly merchants holding up sliced peaches to taste, musicians busting live beats, endless bouquets of flowers, stacks of cheeses, mounds of crabs and salmon resting on shaved ice. Since 1907, the beloved Pike Place Market has been the center for all things beautiful in Seattle. No place awakens an epicurean's senses like one of the oldest public farmers' market in the United States.

The minute you spot the neon sign with the words PUBLIC MARKET and breathe the fragrant air, you feel happier. The magnificence of the produce turns any photographer into a pro. Crowds gather around the fishmongers, grown men acting like boys, tossing salmon into the air. Families take turns posing with the market's unofficial mascot, a bronze pig that goes by the name Rachel.

Downtown Seattle offers many delights, but I suggest you spend at least half a day in the Pike Place Market, moving from stall to stall and purchasing bites to share with the people exploring this lovely waterfront city with you. Stop off for lunch at one of the market restaurants overlooking Elliot Bay. Follow the stairs down to the waterfront—a beautiful area with numerous restaurants and hotels, the Seattle Aquarium, the 9-acre Olympic Sculpture Park, and views that will take your breath away. Nearby, Belltown is a trendy area with hip restaurants and clubs.

Historic Pioneer Square is the oldest part of Seattle, where the city began. South of the Market and near two gigantic sports stadiums, this neighborhood was once a logging center and supply port for gold rushers. Now it's an artsy cultural center of entertainment with many restaurants and gift shops. Salumi, offering specialty Italian meats, is one of the most popular sandwich joints in town. Within walking distance you'll find the Chinatown/International District, where you can sample many kinds of Asian cuisine, from Chinese to Japanese, Vietnamese, and Thai.

You don't really need a car to explore downtown Seattle, where parking spots can be hard to find. Metro buses have a ride-free area in downtown Seattle, extending from the north at Battery Street to South Jackson Street on the south, and east at 6th Avenue to the waterfront on the west. When traveling beyond the ride-free zone, simply pay a small fee when you get off.

This section will show you the gems of downtown Seattle, including Belltown, Central Waterfront, Chinatown/International District, Pike Place Market, and Pioneer Square.

In this chapter you'll find everything from where to eat in the Market to Belltown's favorite hangouts. You'll discover specialty stores that will keep you browsing for hours and bakeries to pick up cakes for any occasion.

We've designated all shops in Pike Place Market with 🐟 (a symbolic representation of the market's famous flying fish).

Made Here

🐟 **Bottega Italiana,** 1425 1st Ave., Seattle, WA 98101; (206) 343-0200; Pike Place Market; www.bottegaitaliana.com. (See website for additional location.) Located in the Pike Place Market is this authentic gelato place. What started as two Italian men reminiscing over their homeland in a conversational Italian class developed into Bottega Italiana, with two locations in Seattle and one in San Diego, California. They use all natural products, including fresh fruit. You might not be able to find your favorite fruit flavor unless it is in season, which is great because it just means that you are getting the best, and of course it makes choosing much easier. They also have dairy-free or vegan options. The most popular flavor is the salted caramel chocolate chip.

Boulangerie Nantaise, 2507 4th Ave., Seattle, WA 98121; (206) 728-1874; Belltown; www.boulangerie-nantaise.com. To step into Boulangerie Nantaise is to step into an actual French bakery. This organic, locally operated "bakery of Nantes" uses levain—a type of pre-ferment—instead of yeast in all their breads. The traditional

preparation gives the bread a denser structure, keeps it fresh longer, and claims to be healthier. Their products are baked fresh daily. Take home a baguette, a savory walnut bread, rustic garlic bread, or let them do the work and grab a house-made sandwich. For those with a sweet tooth, they also have croissants, *pain au chocolat*, apple turnovers, seasonal fruit tarts, and other delectable goodies. Recommended: the almond croissant, twice baked with house-made almond paste. Here is a sweet place to finish work on your computer or for coffee with a friend.

Chukar Cherries, 1529-B Pike Place (center of the main arcade building near the Skybridge Elevator), Seattle, WA 98101; (800) 624-9544; Pike Place Market; www.chukar.com. While perusing through Pike Market, don't miss the Chukar stand. Just ask for a taste, and a plump, chocolate-covered cherry will fill your mouth with joy. In 1988, Pamela Montgomery left her Seattle

HAVE QUESTIONS ABOUT THE PIKE PLACE MARKET?

Stop by the Information Booth at 1st Avenue and Pike Street, pick up a map, and have your questions answered by the friendly staff of the Seattle Convention and Visitors Bureau. Open daily, 10 a.m. to 6 p.m. For more about the Pike Place Market, visit www.pikeplacemarket.org.

marketing job to purchase the largest cherry orchard in Washington and eventually launch Chukar Cherries (named after the chukar, a small game bird found throughout eastern Washington), now an iconic food gift and guilty pleasure for many cherry lovers. JT Montgomery, affectionately called Pa Chukar, is CFO, manager, and cherry lover extraordinaire. Try the Cabernet Chocolate Cherries, Black Forest Chocolate Cherries, or any of the many options in dark or milk chocolate. This is a perfect gift to send to friends and family, and online orders are available. Looking for a day trip? Drive 3 hours east on I-90 and I-82 through the Yakima Valley to Prosser (exit 80), turn right on Wine Country Road, and arrive at the Chukar Cherries Headquarters and Factory Store, a hub of orchards, vineyards, and wineries are nearby.

The Confectional, 1530 Pike Place, Seattle, WA 98101; (206) 282-4422; Pike Place Market; www.theconfectional.com. If the winter in Seattle gets you down, the Golden Girl approach always seems to be convincing—get your friends around a luscious cheesecake and let the stories begin. This tiny cheesecake storefront has a variety of cheesecakes in individual serving sizes made with all-natural products and high-quality ingredients. The most popular flavors are the raspberry white chocolate, Seattle's New York–style cheesecake, and quadruple-chocolate cheesecake. Try the cheesecake truffles—cheesecake batter rolled into balls and dipped in rich Guittard dark chocolate. You can get a variety box

Costco. It all started here....

It's a guilty pleasure for so many of us. Strolling through this enormous warehouse, sampling foods down the aisles and choosing among the big boxes of everything imaginable, it's like being a kid in a candy store. All this started in the Northwest. So when you recognize the Kirkland Signature brand, Costco's store brand, know that it was named after the eastside suburb of Seattle. Costco recently took the plunge in true Northwest fashion and is now committed to improving on seafood and sustainability, and they have agreed to stop selling the red-listed varieties of fish while taking measures to promote sustainable practices. Way to go, Costco! Visit www.costco.com for details.

of 16, giving each person a bite of a different creamy pleasure. Medium and large cheesecakes are available by order only, and all the cakes can be shipped anywhere in the United States. On cold days, treat yourself to a cup of the Colombian hot chocolate made of dark chocolate, organic whole milk, and Columbian coffee and spices. Since there is no seating, grab your cheesecake and sit by the water, overlooking the Pike Place Market.

The Crumpet Shop, 1503 1st Ave., Seattle, WA 98101; (206) 682-1598; Pike Place Market; www.thecrumpetshop.com. When you want a simple breakfast with a side of tea, the Crumpet is the answer. This place is the only crumpet shop in the city. This circular bread sequined with little holes really camouflages itself to reflect the toppings. Savory combinations include smoked salmon, cream cheese, eggs, and pesto. Sweet flavors include generous amounts of Nutella or ricotta and preserves by Washington-made Deer Mountain Berry Farm.

Dahlia Bakery, 2001 4th Ave., Seattle, WA 98121; (206) 441-4540; Belltown; www.tomdouglas.com/restaurants/dahlia-bakery. This place is a shrine for high-quality pastries and breads where renowned restaurateur Chef Tom Douglas takes whatever cravings he has and brings them to life. Located in Belltown not too far from Dahlia Lounge, Serious Pie, Lola, and Palace Kitchen, this bakery has the best triple coconut cream pie in the city, with toasted coconut and just the right balance of sweetness, cream, and crust. Everything I have tried here has been delicious, from the éclairs to the peanut butter cookies and the doughnuts. The bakery is tiny, so be prepared to wait in line—and lines often go out the door. Rustic breads include selections like potato and olive oil, *ficelle,* kalamata olive ciabatta, challah on Friday, and some interesting sandwich combinations. Next time you are running to a potluck, pick up the Lola tzatziki and hummus, some fresh bread and a coconut cream pie. For the frugal readers: Happy hour is Mon to Fri, 4 to 6 p.m. with discounts on selected items, which rotate daily, and on Mondays pie bites are $1.

Daily Dozen Doughnut Co., 93 Pike St.; Seattle, WA 98101; (206) 467-7769; Pike Place Market. A doughnut shop that has been around for over 20 years and still has a line almost all day long. The charm of this place is in its simplicity: fresh, hot mini doughnuts served in a brown paper bag, heating the roof of your mouth on a chilly day, the aroma taunting you as you wait in line. The doughnuts come in dozens or half dozens. The flavors are plain, powdered, cinnamon, or sprinkled (chocolate fudge with sprinkles). The powdered sugar and sprinkled come cold but the other two come hot. Get your doughnut and strategically slip into **Market Spice** (see p. 117) just across the way for a sample of the Market Spice Cinnamon-Orange Tea.

Dry Soda, 410 1st Ave. South, WA 98104; (206) 652-2345 or (888) DRY-SODA; Pioneer Square; www.drysoda.com. Pregnant women and people who do not drink will no longer have to settle for a glass of water. Dry Soda is a beverage that uses all natural ingredients to create a flavorful, caffeine-free, gluten-free, sodium-free alternative to wine with flavors like blood orange, cucumber, juniper berry, and lemongrass. Sharelle Klaus, a mother of four, invented this soda in 2005, because she wanted a beverage that was healthy but that could pair well with fine cuisine. Drop into the tasting room where you can sample all the different flavors. You will not walk out tipsy, guaranteed.

 Beecher's Handmade Cheese

Nothing beats the quintessential Pike Place experience of pressing your head against the glass of **Beecher's Handmade Cheese** (1600 Pike Place, Seattle, WA 98101; 206-956-1964; Pike Place Market; www.beecherscheese.com) to watch cheese being made in front of your eyes. Here you are invited to stare as cheesemakers turn whey to cheese and a metamorphosis takes place. Go inside Beecher's and order some of the "World's Best Mac & Cheese" or creamy tomato soup and a cheese stick while you grab a seat to watch the rest of the cheesemaking experience. Before you leave, sample the large selection of cheeses in the shop, taste some of the famous cheese curds, and take home the signature Flagship cheese, a semi-hard cow's milk cheese that has been aged for one year. They have a few varieties that don't need to be refrigerated and can be shipped or taken on flights. Recommended: Named after Bob Marley's legendary song, No Woman cheese has a spicy kick to it, with Jamaican jerk spices and a touch of brown sugar. Insider tip: Come before 11 a.m. to beat the crowds. See Kurt Beecher Dammeier's recipe for **Golden Beet Risotto** (made with Beecher's cheese) on p. 205.

Fran's Chocolates, 1325 1st Ave., Seattle, WA 98101; (206) 682-0168; Downtown; www.franschocolates.com. For a full description see the North listing, p. 6.

Gelatiamo, 1400 3rd Ave., Seattle, WA 98101; (206) 467-9563; Downtown; www.gelatiamo.com. Oh Gelatiamo—saying the name just makes me smile. Gelatiamo has been serving gelato in downtown Seattle since 1996. Co-owner Maria Coassin, comes from a small town in northern Italy where her family owned a bakery for over 250 years. In an effort to continue the legacy she opened this gelato shop and bakery. Maria and co-owner Skyler Locatelli are always developing new recipes. The most popular flavors are the chocolate and the coconut, but for more-original flavors go for the rice gelato or the Pike Brewery XXXXX chocolate stout gelato. The most talked-about cake is the Dimplomatica, a rum-soaked sponge cake. They also have a selection of gelato cakes that can be custom made for your flavor preference.

Grand Central Bakery, 214 1st Ave. South, Seattle, WA 98104; (206) 622-3644; Pioneer Square; www.grandcentralbakery.com. (See website for additional locations.) Where does the president eat when in town? President Obama's last visit here included a visit to Grand Central Bakery, where he had nothing less than a seasonal spinach salad with Skagit Valley strawberries, a turkey and chutney sandwich, and the must-have Jammer, a flakey biscuit with Oregon's Glenmore Farms jam. With bakeries in Seattle and Portland, Grand Central is dedicated to sustainability and connections with local farmers and producers; they use flour from Shepherd's Grain, eggs from Quilceda Farm, and meat from Thundering Hooves. Bakery treats include items like twice-baked challah, pecan sticky buns, and Irish soda bread. Don't miss their semolina baguettes, a mix of regular wheat flour and durum semolina flour, which can be found at notable restaurants like **Le Pichet** (see p. 128) and **Cafe Campagne** (see p. 125). Drop by one of their bakeries at around 10:30 a.m. and you can score a fresh baguette that was baked just an hour and a half prior. Are you looking for an easy dinner? Their U-Bake line has take-home pizza dough, pie dough, cookies, and puff pastry that you just pop into the oven.

Kukuruza Popcorn, 215 Pike St., Seattle, WA 98101; (206) 623-8000; Downtown; www.kukuruza.com. A popcorn haven, situated just 3 blocks away from the Pike Place Market, you won't be able to miss it if you follow your nose. With over 30 varieties daily, this gourmet popcorn is made of all-natural, wholesome ingredients. It feels much lighter than commercial popcorn, and doesn't leave you with a gritty film under your nails. Try savory combinations like jalapeño cheese, chipotle cheddar cheese, and buffalo blue cheese. For your sweet tooth, try the rocky road or the s'more flavors.

Le Panier, 1902 Pike Place, Seattle, Washington 98101; (206) 441-3669; Pike Place Market; www.lepanier.com. Nothing beats starting your day with a coffee and a croissant in hand. It's even better when your face is pressed against the glass of a window, watching the hustle and bustle of the Pike Place Market and inhaling the perfume of butter and French bread. The selection is exceedingly generous with crusty baguettes, brioches, French macarons, éclairs, croissants, napoleons, fruit tarts, and sandwiches. The lines are long, and it is packed at almost anytime of the day.

Macrina Bakery, 2408 1st Ave.; Seattle, WA 98121; (206) 448-4032; Belltown; www.macrinabakery.com. (See website for additional locations.) Known for its rustic breads made with wholesome ingredients, this bakery and cafe has become an integral part of Seattle's bread culture. Leslie Mackie opened the first Macrina in 1993 with the aim of connecting bread with the communion of sharing that happens over meals. The bakery and cafe has grown substantially since it opened, with three locations and a long list of accolades. Leslie was nominated by the James Beard Foundation for the outstanding pastry chef award numerous times, and Macrina has been voted best bakery by a long list of local publications. The cafe welcomes you with the smell of fresh bread, baguette, challah, brioche, seeded breadsticks, focaccia, brownies, cookies, quiches—and the list

SPOTLIGHT ON SALUMI

Seattlelites are proud of **Salumi Artisan Cured Meats** (309 3rd Ave. South, Seattle, WA 98104; 206-621-8772; Pioneer Square; www.salumicuredmeats.com; $) and with good reason. This Pioneer Square sandwich shop and storefront is the retirement dream of co-founder Armandino Batali. Trained to cure meats in Italy and father to celebrity chef Mario Batali, Armandino spent 31 years as a process control engineer at Boeing before deciding that what he really wanted was to give the Northwest a taste of an Italian *salumeria*. Along with his wife and co-founder Marilyn, the two created an artisan factory that produces incredible cured meats and other Italian foods. In 2003, their daughter Gina Batali and her husband Brian D'Amato bought this iconic establishment, and they have been running and operating it ever since. Busy as it has always has been, the meats are sold in the best restaurants and specialty stores in town. The store is tiny, and the line is always long, sometimes even around the block, but it's worth it to try these handcrafted sandwiches. To avoid the lines, the best time to get there is before they open. Another trick is to order your sandwich in advance and bypass the line to pick it up. For the ultimate Salumi experience, book the private lunch for parties of 8 to 10, Wednesday and Thursday at noon; the price is $40 plus tax, tip, and wine. You can also order the cured meats online to be shipped anywhere in the United States. (***Note:*** Hours are limited, Tues through Fri, 11 a.m. to 4 p.m. But they are committed to making their products fresh every day and will sometimes close earlier if they run out.)

goes on. Be on the look out for the day-old breads at half price, a great option for homemade croutons or toasted sandwiches.

Mee Sum Pastry, 1533 Pike Place, Seattle, WA 98101; (206) 682-6780; Pike Place Market; www.meesum.com. (See website for additional [larger] location.) This tiny, no-frills Cantonese storefront in the Pike Place Market sells fresh pastries like red bean sesame balls, fortune cookies, mini red bean moon cakes, and gigantic almond cookies. The talk of the town is the baked or steamed *humbow,* a huge bun of dough filled with barbecued chicken or pork.

A Piece of Cake, 514–516 S. King St., Seattle, WA 98104; (206) 623-8284; Chinatown/International District; www.apieceofcake seattle.com. This Hong Kong–style bakery has an immense selection of cakes that are light, creamy, and not cloyingly sweet. They have red bean buns, beef buns, barbecue pork buns, taro rolls, red bean pastries, green bean pastries, and lotus pastry with egg yolk—and the list goes on. The bakery is open until 9 p.m., so it's a nice place to fulfill your cravings after a satisfying dinner in the Chinatown/ International District.

Piroshki on 3rd, 710 3rd Ave., Seattle, WA 98104; (206) 322-2820; Downtown; www.piroshkirestaurant.com. For a full description see the Central listing, p. 50.

Piroshky Piroshky, 1908 Pike Place, Seattle, WA 98101; (206) 441-6068; Pike Place Market; www.piroshkybakery.com. On a chilly winter day, wait in line for these Russian turnover-like pastries, inhaling the aroma of butter and cinnamon that fills the street. Watch them roll out the dough right in front of your eyes. When on a walk with friends, get a few pastries for your group (the bakery will cut them up on request) and then sample a bunch as the warm pastry fills your mouth. My top choice here is always the sweet, apple-cinnamon rolls or the cinnamon-cardamom bread. If you prefer savory, anything with potatoes and onions is sure to please. Use the time in line to decide what you want so you don't hold things up when your time to order arrives.

Procopio, 1501 Western Ave., Suite #300, Seattle, WA 98101; (206) 622-4280; Downtown; www.procopiogelati.com. This landmark gelato shop located on the Pike Hillclimb (between Pike Place Market and the Seattle Aquarium) has been around for over 30 years making fresh gelato from scratch with pure ingredients like fruits, nuts, and real liquor. They have authentic flavors like chocolate hazelnut and *stracciatella* (a gelato with a vanilla base and chocolate shavings) as well as more playful flavors that change often, like pineapple basil, blood orange, and strawberry jalapeño.

Starbucks, 1912 Pike Place, Seattle, WA 98101; (206) 448-8762; Pike Place Market; www. Starbucks.com. (See website for additional locations.) This flagship store in Pike Place Market has been here since the early 1970s. The store is tiny (there are no tables or chairs) and charming—it still has the original brown color scheme and Starbucks logo which makes for great photo opportunities. Partners at the registers throw the cups to the baristas much like the fishmongers toss their flying fish. There is no food at this location because of an agreement with the market, but they have plenty of Starbucks memorabilia to take home. Here you can find Pike Place Special Reserve coffee sold in half-pound bags which is only available at this store and at the one up the street at 1st & Pike.

Three Girls Bakery, 1514 Pike Place, Suite 1, Seattle, WA 98101; (206) 622-1045; Pike Place Market. To really get a feel for Pike Place, sit elbow to elbow with the market workers while chomping down on a massive sandwich at this landmark eatery. Since 1912 they've been baking fresh bread and offering lunch for locals and tourists alike. Choose from over 7 varieties of bread with condiment and meat options like corned beef, pastrami, meat loaf, baked salmon, and more. The attached bakery also has a large selection of bread, cookies, croissants, and cakes. Don't miss the classic Reuben sandwich—corned beef,
Swiss cheese, sauerkraut, and Thousand Island dressing grilled between two slices of rye bread. Other location: 6209 15th Ave. Northwest, Seattle, WA 98107; (206) 420-7613; Ballard.

Top Pot Doughnuts, 2124 5th Ave., Seattle, WA 98121; (206) 728-1966; Belltown; www.toppotdoughnuts.com. (See website for additional locations.) This doughnut cafe got its name when two of the co-founders purchased a rusty neon sign atop a Chinese restaurant that said TOP SPOT. The sign was left in their mother's backyard for four years, and when they were finally ready to restore it, the *S* fell off during the ride, and Top Pot was born. This spacious cafe boasts a beautiful window front, book shelves aplenty, modern furniture, and an eclectic crowd of customers from laptop-toting students to families and anyone wanting to savor a good doughnut in a clean and classy atmosphere. The doughnuts, freshly made in small batches, are large in size and fondly referred to as "hand forged." Doughnuts include old-fashioned, cake, rings, bars, sprinkles, and more. Get a variety of doughnuts to go with the coffee that Top Pot roasts and sells.

Uli's Famous Sausage, 1511 Pike Place, Seattle, WA 98101; (206) 838-1712; Pike Place Market; www.ulisfamoussausage .com. While walking through Pike Place Market, stop by this place to pick up sausages for dinner. Owner Uli Lengenberg, a certified sausage meister and butcher, makes sausages at the Georgetown location, without unnatural preservatives or coloring agents. The sausage lineup ranges from pork sausages like Cajun andouille, chorizo picante, or Polish kielbasa to fresh lamb, apple chicken, and rosemary chicken sausages. Take home the merguez, a great combination of lamb, beef, and spices (great for those who don't eat pork). Another favorite is the South African boerewors: pork and

THE HERBFARM

For a magical dining experience, head to **the Herbfarm** (14590 N.E. 145th St., Woodinville, WA 98072; 425-485-5300; www.theherbfarm.com). In this relaxed country bonhomous setting near Seattle, Chef Ron Zimmerman and staff will dazzle your senses with a multicourse meal. This is accomplished through a passion for homegrown and locally foraged ingredients and an attention to detail. The Herbfarm paints a picture of the Pacific Northwest through its dishes made with ingredients and products grown and made in-house. The butter, made from local cream, is churned daily. The breads are fermented with wild yeast and baked in a wood-fired oven. The restaurant makes its own cheeses, cures its own meat from heritage hogs, bakes with eggs laid by their own chickens, and harvests produce daily from its own farm. They also make their own salt.

Dinner at the Herbfarm begins with a tour of the gardens and a peek into the 26,000-bottle wine cellar. The menu is an unfailing 9 courses spanning the flavors of farm, field, forest, and seashore. Six wines accompany the daily fare, or handcrafted nonalcoholic botanicals are available on request. The menu changes roughly every two weeks, offering 26 different "shows" each season. Menu themes span the region: "The Mycologist's Dream," with native mushrooms in October; "A Menu for a Copper King" with Copper River salmon in May; and "An American Harvest" at Thanksgiving, to touch on but a very few. Virtuoso guitarist Patricio Contreras orchestrates the dining room: one moment softly romantic, a passionate rift of "Grenada," a haunting "Blackbird." Stay the night at the Willows Lodge or in one of the Herbfarm's suites. The Herbfarm proves to be an unforgettable evening, an awakening of all the senses.

lamb, red wine vinegar, and coriander. Orders can be made online or by phone. There is a small dining area; order the sausage sampler plate that comes with homemade coleslaw and potato salad, or one of the tasty sandwiches. For a complete list of retailers selling Uli's products, check the website.

Yellow Leaf Cupcakes Co., 2209 4th Ave., Seattle, WA 98121; (206) 441-4240; Belltown; www.theyellowleafcupcake.com. Cupcakes are everywhere. A large majority of Yellow Leaf's cupcakes are frosted with Italian buttercream, an egg white–based cream that is less sugary than traditional buttercream. The cupcakes here change often, giving the regular cupcake seeker a refreshing element of surprise. Find flavors like salted caramel cheesecake, crème brûlée, Washington lavender, classic red velvet, and white chocolate pretzel. The most popular cupcake is pancakes and bacon. Order your cupcakes, and they will deliver free anywhere in Seattle.

Yummy House Bakery, 522 6th Ave. South, Seattle, WA 98104; (206) 340-9308; Chinatown/International District; and Uwajimaya Food Court, 600 5th Ave. South, Seattle, WA 98104; (206) 624-624. The name is self-explanatory. This Hong Kong–style bakery in the International District has a vast selection of authentic pastries. Find coconut tarts, almond cookies, fruit cakes, cream buns, and more. They also have full cakes and wedding cakes. One of the popular items is the paper cupcake, a light and soft sponge cake shaped like an ice-cream cone. They even have a green tea variation.

 **Bavarian Meat Products,** 1920 Pike Place, Seattle, WA 98101; (206) 441-0942; Pike Place Market, www.bavarianmeats .com. This jewel of a specialty store sells a large selection of imported German products such as cookies and snacks, as well as a selection of German sausage, bratwurst, smoked brats, and cheese. They also have imported chocolates and holiday specialty sweets. On Tuesday through Saturday, get fresh *Brötchen,* German rolls and fresh pretzels.

The Chocolate Box, 108 Pine St., Seattle, WA 98101; (206) 443-3900; Downtown; www.sschocolatebox.com. This locally owned chocolate shop carries an extensive line of chocolates from local companies such as **Theo Chocolate, Oh! Chocolate, Fran's Chocolates, Fiori Chocolate,** and more. They serve **Caffé Vita** coffee along with some baked goods and gelato. Gluten-free heads up: They carry a couple gluten-free bakery items, such as the brownies from **Louisa's Cafe & Bakery** and **Vivir** chocolate, which is also dairy free. There is a small seating area inside and some outdoor seating. Recommended: hot chocolate in the winter, and for the summer, frozen hot chocolate made with European sipping chocolate and blended gelato. A perfect gift for the chocolate lover, the Chocolate Indulgence Tour by **Savor Seattle Food Tours** will take you on a two-hour walking tour through the city for $49, complemented with decadent sweets galore. Continue next door to **106 Pine** (106 Pine St., Seattle, WA 98101; 206-443-1106; www.106pine.com), a sleek wine bar, under the same ownership, offering local cheeses and lovely bites with Northwest wines.

The Chocolate Market, 1906 Post Alley, Seattle, WA 98101; (206) 443-0505; Pike Place Market. This romantic chocolate store is what chocolate dreams are made of. Antique furniture, dreamy displays, and a broad selection of candies and local chocolates like **Oh! Chocolate** (see p. 50), **Vivir,** and more. A big attraction is the enormous chair that looks like it came out of the Three Bears story with a sign that says AMONG LIFE'S MYSTERIES IS HOW A TWO-POUND BOX OF CHOCOLATES CAN MAKE A WOMAN GAIN 5 POUNDS. The welcoming feel and quaint seating area is ideal for love birds sharing a decadent chocolate truffle or visitors having a post-market snack. During the winter, curl up with a hot chocolate topped with fluffy artisan marshmallows.

City Fish Co., 1535 Pike Place, Seattle, WA 98101; (800) 334-2669; Pike Place Market; www.cityfish.com. Since 1917, this landmark has been a great place for halibut, salmon, crab, and high-quality seafood. Loved by locals and tourists alike, friendly service and quality is what you get. The emphasis here is on the experience of the staff, really willing to help, giving advice and catering to your needs. They offer free delivery to the downtown hotels.

DeLaurenti Specialty Food & Wine, 1435 1st Ave., Seattle, WA 98101; (206) 622 -0141; Pike Place Market; www.delau

renti.com. DeLaurenti is a top-notch Italian food and wine specialty shop located a few steps from the fish throwers at the Pike Place Market. They have over 250 cheeses to choose and sample. They have many varieties of charcuterie, house-made antipasto salads, and a large selection of breads to choose from. They have a vast assortment of chocolates, cookies, condiments, and grains, and a small dining area with pizza, sandwiches, baked goods, and salads. If you are on a hunt for quality olive oil, browse through the large selection of olive oils from around the world, and don't miss their extensive wine collection. Here you will find those cookies or imported products that you have been looking for all over. Also, ask about the fresh pasta behind the counter. Choose something from the cheese counter and get a crunchy baguette for a quick picnic by the water.

Don and Joe's Meats, 85 Pike St., Seattle, WA 98101; (206) 682-7670; Pike Place Market; www.donandjoesmeats.com. Don Jr. might not be the original Don behind the name of this butcher counter, but like his father, he continues to provide the best meats and customer service. Founded by his father, Don, and his Uncle Joe in 1969, this place has been the one-stop butcher for all the meats including hard-to-find items like lamb tongues and beef or veal sweetbreads. They also carry prime and natural beef and a full selection of lamb and veal, as well as Rocky Mountain oysters, ducks, rabbits, and hanger and skirt steaks. Sausages are made in-house. If you are interested in ordering whole pigs or whole lambs, give them a call at least a week in advance.

El Mercado Latino, 1514 Pike Place, # 6, Seattle WA 98101; (206) 623-3240; Pike Place Market; www.latinmerchant.com. Rows of hanging peppers will lead you to this small specialty shop that carries a generous selection of hard-to-find Latin foods and food-related products. With products like *dulce de leche,* Spanish saffron, passion fruit and guava concentrates, Lizano sauce, Harina P.A.N corn flour used for *arepas,* and more. You can find anything you need for an authentic Spanish meal. Pick up some of the Mexican candies for a sweet treat.

Jack's Fish Spot, 1514 Pike Place, #2, Seattle, WA 98101; (206) 467-0514; Pike Place Market; www.jacksfishspot.com. Opened in 1981 by Jack Mathers, this popular spot is a sight for hungry eyes: You will find live seafood swimming around in tanks in the middle of the Pike Place Market. Choose from items like Quilcene oysters, Penn Cove mussels, Manila clams, sockeye king or silver salmon, and house-made alderwood-smoked salmon. Then grab a seat and order some Dungeness crab cooked in Jack's crab cooker, fish-and-chips, Northwest-style clam chowder, halibut, scallops, prawns, or steamed clams and mussels. Jack still manages to be there all the time. Don't miss a true Seattle and Pike Place Market experience.

King's Barbecue House, 518 6th Ave. South, Seattle, WA 98104; (206) 622-2828; Chinatown/International District; and 303 12th Ave. South, Seattle, WA 98144; (206) 720-4715; Chinatown/ International District. This hole-in-the-wall Chinese barbecue shop is an avid carnivore's dream. You'll recognize the place by the succulent roast ducks, chickens, and pork hanging in the store window. King's has been serving this area for over 20 years. Locals love the glazed, crackly skin on the roasted poultry and the sweet and savory flavors of the barbecued pork. The portions are large and very affordable.

La Buona Tavola, 1524 Pike Place, Seattle, WA 98101; (206) 292-5555; Pike Place Market; www.trufflecafe.com. If the thought of truffles—those rare, aromatic mushrooms—makes you go weak in the knees, you'd better brace yourself for this truffle cafe. This tiny Italian specialty food and wine shop is a must stop when strolling through the Pike Place Market. The owner, known as the Truffle Queen, staffs her shop with the sweetest people around, who delight in having you taste and browse through their wonderful sample table, loaded with truffles in every form: white and black truffle oils, creams, sauces, honey—and their 10 percent– concentration truffle salt. Don't miss the experience of tasting their sweet, rich, aged balsamics, as well as the delicious sauces and condiments that will turn even the simplest grilled cheese sandwich or scrambled eggs into a delicacy. If you are ready to splurge, ask for the real deal: fresh truffles imported from Italy, available seasonally, and priced reasonably (especially in summer and fall, when they're the least expensive). Stop by any afternoon and enjoy a wine tasting—3 wines for just $5, definitely a steal—or go to one of their monthly evening wine events. Shipping is available anywhere in the United States and most other countries abroad; online orders of $50 or more ship free within the United States.

Lam's Seafood Market, 1221 S. King St., Seattle, WA 98144; (206) 720-0969; Chinatown/International District. It's not only about the seafood. Yes they do have a large variety of seafood at great prices—fish tanks full of it—but they also have produce, noodles, tofu, and all the other specialty items you need to cook a complete Asian dinner. This place is certainly no-frills and bustling with people, but if you want to get the goods and save money, then this is your place.

Marie & Freres, 2122 Westlake Ave., Seattle, WA 98121; (206) 859-3534; Belltown; www.marieandfreres.com. Dark chocolate lovers will keel over at this chocolate specialty shop carrying Claudio Corallo Chocolates. Chocolate virtuoso Claudio Corallo began his journey growing coffee in the middle of the Congo. He later moved to the volcanic archipelago of Sao Tome and Principe, where he cultivated the descendants of the very first cacao plants that, in 1819, arrived in Africa from the distant shores of South America. It seems unreal, in this age of giant agribusiness, that family farmers of this sort still exist, but they do, and the result is an extraordinary line of chocolates, with bars up to 100 percent cocoa. Try the *gengibre* made with crystallized ginger or *laranja,* the ultimate combination of citrus and chocolate. The 100 percent cocoa is described by the website as "having an incredibly long finish similar to a very bold, dry Cabernet." This is *the* one bite of chocolate you want after a really good dinner.

Market Spice, 85-A Pike Place, Seattle, WA 98101; (206) 622-6340; Pike Place Market; www.marketspice.com. If you like cooking, this will be your guilty pleasure. This 100-year-old spice shop has over 240 spices and blends from the most basic to the rare and exotic. Spices can be purchased by the ounce, allowing you to experiment without breaking the bank. Have a sample of the Market Spice Cinnamon-Orange Tea, a fruity blend of orange, cinnamon, and cloves. Sip your sample as you ask a million questions about every spice on the wall. For the tea lover, there are just about as many tea blends as there are spices and a huge variety of tea-related collectibles.

Mexican Grocery, 1914 Pike Place, Seattle, WA 98101; (206) 441-1147; Pike Place Market. You might just miss this tiny hole-in-the-wall Mexican grocery store at first glance, but keep looking because you will find it. They have specialty Mexican products to take home, such as spices, condiments, and sauces. They also have fresh corn and flour tortillas and some tasty homemade items like tamales, burritos, beans, and salsa. They are closed on Sunday and only accept cash or checks.

Oriental Mart, 1506 Pike Place, Seattle, WA 98101; (206) 622-8488; Pike Place Market. This Filipino specialty store carries a huge selection of basic Asian staples, some harder-to-find ingredients, and lots of knickknacks and gift items. This market also serves traditional Filipino food. No fanciness here, but step in the back for some home-cooked food with menu items like their flavorsome fish *sinigang,* a sour soup made with salmon collar purchased fresh from the market. They also have chicken adobo, pork adobo, chili beans, and daily specials.

Paris Grocery, 1418 Western Ave., Seattle, WA 98101; (206) 682-0679; www.parisgroceryseattle.com. When you're craving some Parisian charm, stop by this petite specialty store by the owners of the gorgeous **Spanish Table** (a few stores down the street; see p. 121). They carry a variety of quality French cheeses, flavorful pâtés, chocolates, and hard-to-find French specialties. Some interesting finds are their large selection of mustards, cured pork belly, duck leg confit, and canned duck *foie gras.* Don't miss the selection of French wines at reasonable prices.

Pike Place Creamery, 1514 Pike Place, Suite #3; Seattle, WA 98101; (206) 622-5029; Pike Place Market. Before supermarkets, you'd get your bread from the baker, meat from the butcher, and your milk from the creamery. Give yourself the pleasure of walking into a shop where you don't just get to choose the size of your milk carton but which local farm it comes from. There are half a dozen varieties of milk to choose from and eggs that you can mix and match; their selection ranges from chicken to duck, quail, and turkey and goose eggs seasonally. They also have vegan products as well as cheeses, yogurts, butters, and other dairy items. For the kitsch collector, udders and cows of every shape and size are featured in the form of candies, cookies, toys, and even galoshes. This place will meet all your dairy requirements for the day and possibly the week.

Pike Place Fish Market, 86 Pike Place, Seattle, WA 98101; (206) 682-7181; Pike Place Market; www.pikeplacefish.com. It has become an icon for Seattle, fish leaping into the air, while the crew chants at the top of their lungs. Tourists and locals have to encounter the kiss of the flying fish at one point in their life. Join in and take your photos with this rowdy crew of fish slingers, and don't forget Rachel the pig, the bronze statue in the middle of it all. More than just a Seattle landmark, Pike Place Fish offers a huge selection of seafood and a knowledgeable and playful crew, always ready to answer your questions. They can ship to anywhere in the

United States and can pack the fish to stay cold for 1 or 2 days. If you like to avoid the crowds, fish is also available for order online.

Pure Food Fish Market, 1511 Pike Place, Seattle, WA 98101; (206) 622-5765; Pike Place Market; www.freshseafood.com. Locals come in to get fish advice from Sol Amon because nobody knows the subject like Sol, who was been working here since his father opened the place in 1956. His father is no longer around, but Sol owns the place, and four generations of the family work at this market. This store, located in the middle of the market, offers a tremendous selection of seafood: high-quality fish as well as crabs, scallops, lobster tails, prawns, and other shellfish. They also have smoked salmon, caviar, and cold, fresh smoked lox that you can have sliced as thick (or thin) as you want. For a fee, they will pack the fish in a box that will keep it fresh for 48 hours. You can order fish online as well.

Quality Cheese, 1508 Pike Place, Seattle, WA 98101; (206) 624-4029; Pike Place Market. Sometimes, you just want to buy cheese at a place that specializes in just that. Pike Place Market's old-fashioned cheese counter is jam-packed with a large variety of cheese at great prices.

The Souk, 1916 Pike Place, Seattle, WA 98101; (206) 441-1666; Pike Place Market. Hidden in the abundance of the Pike Place

Market is this 30-year-old gem of a store, filled with Arabic and Indian products, accessories, and trinkets. A "souk" is a commercial quarter or marketplace, and the Souk offers wide-ranging selections from imported Indian crackers and chips to hard-to-find spices, beans, and trinkets like brassy bells and whistles from the Middle East. Poke around and ask questions; the owner is eager to explain. Pick up a chunk of the Lebanese halvah, a rich Middle Eastern dessert made of ground sesame; or some *labneh,* a thick yogurt cheese; along with some *za'atar,* a blend of herbs made of dried sumac, sesame seeds, and other spices. When you get home, spread the *labneh* on a round plate, drizzle with some olive oil and, sprinkle with generous amounts of the *za'atar* spice. Dip bread or pita in it.

The Spanish Table, 1426 Western Ave., Seattle, WA 98101; (206) 682-2827; Downtown; www.spanishtable.com. If you like cooking Spanish food or experimenting with new flavors, this spacious Spanish specialty shop carries food products to assist in that endeavor. They carry over 900 Spanish and Portuguese wines, over a dozen types of chorizo, a large selection of cheese and hard-to-find items like squid ink, *padron* peppers, and grey mullet botargo (cured fish roe). Pick from a large selection of paella pans and cookbooks to recreate the Spanish experience at home. Be sure to ask about books on sale, some listed under $15. This shop is located right behind the Pike Place Market so make sure not to miss it on your market expedition. When you are done shopping, walk a few stores down to the other shop by the same owner, **Paris Grocery** (see p. 118).

Uwajimaya Market, 600 5th Ave. South, #100, Seattle, WA 98104; (206) 624-6248; Chinatown/International District; www.uwajimaya .com. (See website for additional locations.) After returning from a Japanese internment camp in California at the end of World War II, the Moriguchi family relocated to Seattle and reopened the Uwajimaya Market. Family members still manage the market, which  has expanded to surrounding cities. Visit the market to discover Asian housewares and specialties, imported snacks, noodles, teas, fresh fish, and reasonably priced Asian vegetables. The Chinatown/International District Uwajimaya has a bookstore and a food court with a large variety of food options. Parking will be validated for an hour of shopping if you spend over $7.50, or $15 for 2 hours. This is a great place for browsing and discovering new foods.

Viet Wah Supermarket, 1032 S. Jackson St., Seattle, WA 98104; (206) 329-1399; Chinatown/International District; visit www .vietwah.com. (See website for additional locations.) Where you shop has much to do about your style and what you are willing to look through. Like clothes, some like it organized and some love wading through the racks of bargains. Viet Wah is the latter, an Asian market that has all the specialty foods you need to create a good meal: duck eggs, quail eggs, the noodles, the seafood, the ingredients. It is no Uwajimaya—it lacks the glamour of that store—but it definitely has its own charm and great prices.

World Spice Merchants, 1509 Western Ave., Seattle, WA 98101; (206) 682-7274; Downtown; www.worldspice.com. Located behind the Pike Place Market, this roomy spice store is as much an experience as it is a shop. Take the time to absorb the scents of all the spices and discover spice blends that you have never heard of. Here there are choices to make. Since the spices are ground to order, you can decide if you want them fine or coarse, in a sealed bag or in a jar. They will also custom blend spices for you. While waiting for your order to be processed, the staff behind the counter can give you tips and ideas. They also have a nice selection of teas and cookbooks. Recommended: Mayan cocoa and Seattle Salmon Rub. Online orders available; check the website for more information. See World Spice Merchants' recipe for **Caramelized Apples with Seattle Six Spice & Alder Smoked Salt** on p. 192.

Food Lovers' Faves

Bisato, 2400 1st Ave., Seattle, WA 98121; (206) 443-3301; Belltown; www.bisato.com; $. Bisato, the Venetian word for "eel," is the name of this slick Belltown restaurant. It has a circular bar open-air kitchen where Chef Scott Carsberg can be found creating masterpieces of food for you to devour, all in a casual yet sophisticated atmosphere. The food is served on small plates giving you the chance to sample haute, modernist cuisine at more affordable prices. Bisato works just as well for a night out with light bites and drinks or for a classy multicourse dinner. Reservations can be made for 5 or more, and minors are not allowed. Reserve the semiprivate room for parties up to 10.

Blueacre Seafood, 1700 7th Ave., Seattle, WA; 98101; (206) 659-0737; Downtown; http://blueacreseafood.com; $$$. Seafood lovers rejoice: This all American seafood restaurant, located in the heart of downtown Seattle, sources sustainably farmed freshwater species, oysters, clams, and a large selection of wild seafood. It's the second restaurant of Chef Kevin and Terresa Davis, owners of **Steelhead Diner** (see p. 133)— spacious and modern with a full oyster bar, 3 private dining rooms, and an all-American wine list. Open for lunch and dinner daily as well as for weekend brunch. Happy hour is available in the lounge daily from 3 to 6 p.m. Recommended items: seafood and andouille gumbo, olive-crusted Alaskan halibut, and the jumbo lump Dungeness crab cake.

BuiltBurger, 217 James St., Seattle, WA 98104; (206) 724-0599; Pioneer Square; www.builtburger.com; $. Nestled in the heart and soul of Pioneer Square, BuiltBurger is the only gourmet burger destination downtown. It's not your traditional burger fare. Think big, bold flavors captured inside grass-fed patties like Sriracha Beef, Supreme Pastrami, and Magnificent Chorizo. They are the kind of burgers that can stand alone, without the bun. A visit isn't complete without an order of piping-hot savory beignets, flecked with Bloody Mary salt from a local artisan company, Secret Stash Sea Salts. Also on tap are **Trophy Cupcakes** (see p. 13), a rotating assortment of fresh salads, beer, wine, and BuiltDips like smoked chipotle, Chinese mustard, remoulade, and harissa-curry ketchup.

Cafe Campagne, 1600 Post Alley, Seattle, WA 98101; (206) 728-2233; Pike Place Market; $$; and **Campagne,** 86 Pine St., Seattle, WA 98101; (206) 728-2800; www.campagnerestaurant.com; $$$. Cafe Campagne is one of my favorite places to grab lunch in the market. Situated in Post Alley right below Campagne restaurant, this romantic French cafe has a charm like no other. Grab a seat outside and watch the people pass you by, or sit inside at the bistro-style tables or long wooden bar. Enjoy the lively atmosphere and impressive service. The brunch is a wonderful way to spend a morning, and lunch and dinner are perfect for a business meeting or a romantic date. Recommended: burger d'agneau, a lamb burger with grilled balsamic onions, roasted red peppers, aïoli, and pommes frites. Every Bastille Day (July 14) they have a street party, with wine, beer, street food, and live music and entertainment. For special occasions, head upstairs to Campagne where Chef Daisley Gordon has raised the bar with his ability to use the best ingredients and create top-quality French food.

Cafe Yarmarka, 1530 Post Alley, Suite 3A, Seattle, WA 98101; (206) 521-9054; Pike Place Market; $. The first place I head when I want home-cooked food is a no-frills Russian restaurant nestled in the alley of Pike Place Market. Order the stuffed cabbage rolls, filled with beef, doused in sauce, and covered with a dollop of sour cream, or the *pelemeni*, fluffy dumplings filled with meat and covered with onions. They have a nice selection of creamy Russian salads, coleslaw, and soups that change daily. I once made the "mistake" of bringing a Russian friend from out of town who was staying here, and she refused to eat anywhere else for the rest of the trip.

Elliot Bay Cafe (no bookstore), 103 S. Main St., Seattle, WA 98104; (206) 682-6664; Pioneer Square; www.elliottbaycafe.com; $. For a full description see the Central listing, p. 68.

FareStart, 700 Virginia St., Seattle, WA 98101; (206) 267-7601; Belltown; www.farestart.org; $. This nonprofit restaurant provides opportunities for homeless and disadvantaged individuals to train in the culinary field for job training and placement programs; students learn cooking skills, barista skills, and other food service skills. Open for lunch, Mon through Fri, from 11 a.m. to 2 p.m., and for their unique Guest Chef Night dinners on Thurs, from 6 to 8 p.m. For this special event, well-known local chefs donate their time and ingredients to prepare a memorable dining experience, along with community members from local companies who also volunteer their time. This

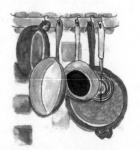

3-course meal costing $24.95 is a true charitable cause: 100 percent of the proceeds and gratuities from Guest Chef Night go back into the program and help to fund student services and training.

Green Leaf, 418 8th Ave. South, Seattle, WA 98104; (206) 340-1388; Chinatown/International District; www.greenleaftaste.com; $$. Locals are infatuated with this cozy, two-level Vietnamese restaurant. The food is traditional Vietnamese with menu items like pho, a rich noodle soup; *bánh xèo,* savory Vietnamese pancakes; and lots of vermicelli and rice dishes.

Hing Loon, 628 S. Weller St., Seattle, WA 98104; (206) 682-2828; Chinatown/International District; $. This no-frills restaurant with cafeteria-style seating, Formica tables, and old chairs is a gem of a place with a never-ending Cantonese menu and tasty items like handmade dumplings, seafood hot pots, congee with doughnuts, and salt-and-pepper tofu, just to name a few. Service is friendly, and the food is inexpensive. Hungry night owls will love the late hours, open Sun through Thurs until 1 a.m., and Fri and Sat until 2 a.m.

Lecōsho, 89 University St. (the Harbor Steps), Seattle, WA 98101; (206) 623-2101; Downtown; www.lecosho.com; $$. Take the Harbor Steps, in the heart of downtown, to Lecōsho, a charming restaurant with an open-air kitchen and rustic touches, from the butcher-block countertop to the copper pans dangling from the ceiling above. Open for lunch and dinner, 7 days a week, Lecōsho is a casual affair by day, with large windows letting in the light and a view of the

Alaskan Way viaduct; in the evenings, the restaurant transforms into an elegant space, twinkling with candlelight. Lecōsho, Chinook jargon for "swine," has lots of plays on the pig, with dishes like *porchetta* and house-brined pork chops, but the fresh seafood and vegetarian items shine just as well. Their meat is butchered in-house, and all the charcuterie is handmade by Chef Mike Easton and his team. Lecōsho takes sustainability one-step further by sending all kitchen scraps across Puget Sound to Vashon Island to feed four pigs that the restaurant is raising.

Le Pichet, 1933 1st Ave., Seattle, WA 98101; (206) 256-1499; Pike Place Market; www.lepichetseattle.com; $$. Just 2 blocks from the fish throwers lies a charming French cafe with authentic food, an inviting space, and outdoor seating during warm summer nights. Quaint enough to read your favorite libertine novel at the 10-seat bar, yet buzzing enough for a night out with some drinks, the atmosphere transports you to a night in Paris. Enjoy house-made charcuterie served alongside Grand Central Bakery baguette, winter soups, and cheese plates. Order the *poulet rôti a votre commande,* chicken roasted to order, available year-round with seasonal sides. This succulent chicken dinner (for 2) takes an hour to make, so start with a *pichet* (jug) of *vin,* the refreshing *salade verte,* and a half-dozen oysters with mignonette sauce and grilled chipolata sausage. Enjoy live music on Sunday (check website for details and a schedule) and don't miss the annual Bastille Day party on July 14, when Le Pichet is full of people, live music, and a grand atmosphere that'll make you want to shout "Vive La France!"

Lola, 2000 4th Ave., Seattle, WA 98121; (206) 441-1430; Belltown; www.tomdouglas.com/restaurants/lola; $$$. Named after Jackie Cross's grandmother, who married a Greek immigrant, this roomy restaurant embodies the warmth of the Mediterranean with eclectic flavors that extend all the way to North Africa. The open door across from the circular bar reveals the lounge area of Hotel Andra, a modern boutique hotel, and ensures the colorful attitudes of guests from swanky out-of-towners to loving locals. Open for breakfast, lunch, dinner, and late-night bites daily. Start with the fresh pita and the spreads, with options like the roasted sweet pepper, cauliflower-anchovy, skordalia-garlic spread, and cows' milk–yogurt tzatziki. Recommended: Anderson Valley lamb burger and chickpea fries or Grandma Dot's Greek Spaghetti, buttery al dente noodles with crispy breadcrumbs.

Long Provincial, 1901 2nd Ave., Seattle, WA 98101; (206) 443-6266; Downtown; www.longprovincial.com; $$. From the owners of **Tamarind Tree** (see p. 133), this Vietnamese restaurant is located just a few blocks from the Pike Place Market. Dimmed lights, soft music, minimalistic decor, and a live jellyfish tank known as the Jelly Bar create an inviting atmosphere that matches the delightful food. The menu is extensive, and the appetizers unique. Recommended: the Turmeric Fish Roll (a salad roll filled with turmeric-marinated catfish, fresh herbs, and rice noodles) and Cinnamon Pork Rice Balls (cinnamon ground pork coated with early-harvested green rice, which is deep-fried and served with tamarind fish sauce).

PAGLIACCI PIZZA

A landmark pizza parlor since 1979, Pagliacci Pizza is where you go to get a slice of good pizza fast. Slices are large and generous on the cheese. Local ingredients like **Salumi Artisan-Cured Meats** (see p. 104) and seasonal mushrooms from **Foraged and Found Edibles** give these pies the Seattle oomph to make them classics. Ask about the seasonal pizzas. The Pagliaccio Salad is a delicious accompaniment for any slice. Customer service is top-notch, and locations can be found all over the city (www.pagliacci .com).

Portfolio Restaurant, Art Institute of Seattle, 2600 Alaskan Way, 5th floor, Seattle WA 98121; (206) 239-2363; Belltown/Waterfront; www.artinstitutes.edu/seattle/about/portfolio-restaurant.aspx; $.

A brisk walk from the Pike Place Market reveals a hidden gem: a restaurant with classic white tablecloths and a breathtaking view of Elliott Bay. The chefs and servers are culinary students from Seattle's Art Institute gaining hands-on experience. Guests are invited to enjoy a 3-course dinner for $19 plus tax. Gratuity is not accepted, but donations to the scholarship fund are welcomed. The menu changes seasonally, and local Washington wines are available for purchase by the glass or bottle. The schedule is tricky: it's only open during school hours; be sure to call and make reservations. The best bet is to come at least a few days into the quarter, when the students have figured things out. *Note:* Call to inquire about the wine tastings by sommelier and restaurant manager, Dieter Schafer, that include 6 wines for $12 on Friday evenings.

Seatown SeaBar & Rotisserie, 2010 Western Ave., Seattle, WA 98121; (206) 436-0390; Pike Place Market; http://tomdouglas.com/index.php/restaurants/seatown; $$. Seatown is everything you've ever wanted in the city: a great location, imaginative riffs on the city's iconic seafood, and quick service. It is an updated lunch counter for Seattle's busiest tourist intersection at the south end of the Pike Place Market. Roll up your sleeves and pull up a stool at the bar so you can get the ultimate view: chefs carving circles with avocado, pumping blini batter into skillets, or you might even catch a chef using a crème brûlée torch on lemons. The menu concept is simple: creative takes on fresh seafood and rotisserie meats rotating next door, all married with the best produce in the market. On the run? Stop by the rotisserie and grab a sandwich made with the succulent meat of the day, or try one of the classic favorites such as the roasted chicken, short ribs, or *porchetta*. See Chef Tom Douglas's recipe for **Jackie's Tomatoes with Avocado Skordalia** on p. 190.

Serious Pie, 316 Virginia St., Seattle, WA 98121; (206) 838-7388; Belltown; http://tomdouglas.com/index.php/restaurants/serious -pie; $$. Seriously. This is where you get serious pizza. It took three months for Chef Gwen Leblanc to figure out the formula for this pizza crust—lightly crispy on the edges and soft and delicate on the inside—which is baked in a stone-cased, apple-wood-burning oven for 7 to 9 minutes at 680 degrees. The toppings range from combinations like buffalo mozzarella and San Marzano tomato; Penn Cove clams, house pancetta, and lemon thyme; or sweet fennel sausage with roasted peppers. The bistro-style atmosphere and communal tables make this place a fun, casual eating experience with top-notch food. Waits may be long during the evening but well worth it; beat the crowds by coming a little later or take advantage of happy hour from 3 to 5 p.m. on weeknights when all pies are $5. There is a second location in Westlake (see p. 81).

Spur Gastropub, 113 Blanchard St., Seattle, WA 98121; (206) 728-6706; Belltown; www.spurseattle.com; $$. Young and innovative are the key words describing this compact yet swanky Belltown gastropub. Chef-owners Brian McCracken and Dana Tough have been praised for their playfulness in the kitchen by *GQ* magazine, *Conde Nast Traveler,* Gayot.com, and *Food & Wine*'s "Go List." Expect small plates with touches of molecular gastronomy and playful flavor combinations. This vibrant duo also own **Tavern Law** (see p. 82), a bar located on Capitol Hill. Try the 3-course tasting menu for $45. Recommended: pork belly sliders and grass-fed beef burger. Twenty-one and over. See Spur's recipe for **Microwaved Chocolate Sponge Cake** on p. 214.

 **Steelhead Diner,** 95 Pine St., Seattle, WA 98101; (206) 625-0129; Pike Place Market; www.steelheaddiner.com; $$$. This foxy diner is one of those go-to restaurants where locals like to hang out and tourists like to visit. Some of my best conversations have unfolded here while nibbling on a snack at the bar, after a day of shopping with my girlfriends. The diner is casual, fashionable, and buzzing with energy. The food is a gathering of comfort food using the bountiful seafood and local ingredients of the Pike Place Market. Don't miss a seat on the patio overlooking Post Alley or a seat with a view through the windows. Order the *poutine,* crispy fries topped with gravy, Beecher's cheese curds, and the crab cakes.

Tamarind Tree, 1036 S. Jackson St., Suite A, Seattle, WA 98104; (206) 860-1404; Chinatown/International District; www.tamarind treerestaurant.com; $$. This diamond in the rough is hidden at the end of a small strip mall in the International District. Walk inside and find a lively Vietnamese restaurant with a stylish take on bona-fide Vietnamese food. Enjoy items like Tamarind Tree Rolls (salad rolls with fresh herbs, fried tofu, roasted peanut, fresh coconut, jicama, and carrots), steamed coconut rice cakes, Tamarind Tree Crêpes, or specialty noodle soups. Try the flavorful fruit-infused sodas with your meals for an interesting kick. Service is friendly, prices are inexpensive, and the place is always busy, so prepare to wait. Recommended: Order the 7 courses of beef.

TASTE Restaurant, 1300 1st Ave.; Seattle, WA 98101; (206) 903-5291; Downtown; www.tastesam.com/restaurant; $$$. While museum food may not always be something to write home about, the food at TASTE Restaurant, located in the Seattle Art Museum, really sets this place apart. The emphasis here is on local ingredients, sustainability, and classic techniques merged with the best seasonal produce. In fact, they source their ingredients from over 50 farm-to-fork local companies. Open for lunch and dinner Tues through Sat and brunch on Sun. You won't want to miss the happy hour menus with $5 items and oysters at $1.50 a piece. Happy hour recommended: the Alsatian-style flatbread. For the ultimate deal, drop in on the first Thursday of the month, when entrance to the Seattle Art Museum (along with some other local museums) is free. TASTE is also known for its 100 percent Northwest wine list as well as its focus on pairing food and wine together. Before you order at TASTE, ask about the "flight and bites" tasting menu where you get 3 bites with 3 small wine tastings for $16.

Tavolata, 2323 2nd Ave., Seattle, WA 98121; (206) 838-8008; Belltown; www.ethanstowellrestaurants.com; $$. Chef Ethan Stowell's Tavolata captures the beauty of Italian dining. Tavolata is around the table dining: a large communal table across the dining room, an open kitchen so you can peek inside as they hand craft pasta, and a rustic yet modern design. Cozy and warm, Tavolata is the ideal atmosphere for breaking bread, talking, and enjoying wine with your dinner. Recommended: For dessert, order the *zeppole* doughnuts. See Chef Ethan Stowell's recipe for **Gnocchetti with Pancetta, Spring Onions & English Peas** on p. 196.

Thai Curry Simple, 406 5th Ave. South, Seattle, WA 98104; (206) 327-4838; Chinatown/International District; www.thaicurrysimple.com; $. If a busy schedule drives you on the fast-food path, make sure it is good, healthy, and cheap. This Thai restaurant and specialty shop has a long list of curries for under $5 as well as a rotating menu of daily curries for each day of the week. First you order off the menu that is on the wall and then grab a seat. While waiting, you can browse through the selection of specialty products and take-home curries. Mind the sign that says WE DO NOT ADD A STAR FOR SPICINESS, OUR STAR IS IN THE JAR ON THE TABLE, otherwise saying just reach over and add hot sauce to your food. The food has no MSG, and they sell a large selection of Thai beverages. For dessert, try the Thai roti, a pan-fried pastry resembling a crepe with sweet

SPOTLIGHT ON CHEF AND RESTAURATEUR TOM DOUGLAS

Tom Douglas is in a league of his own when it comes to Seattle restaurants. Tom has put Northwest cuisine on the map with his dedication to the ingredients and bounty that is found here, in addition to the involvement with the community. With his wife and business partner, Jackie Cross, the two have filled many niches in the food world, making things happen with their eclectic food establishments such as **Dahlia Lounge** (see p. 140), **Dahlia Bakery** (see p. 98), **Dahlia Workshop** (see p. 3), **Lola** (see p. 129), **Serious Pie** (see p. 132), **Etta's** (see p. 141), **Seatown** (see p. 131), **Palace Kitchen** (see p. 145), and the event and catering space known as the **Palace Ballroom.** Chef Tom Douglas has also published cookbooks, owns a kitchenware line, and has created Rub with Love spice rubs, which can be found in stores nationwide. No matter how busy Tom Douglas may be, you will still find him dining in local restaurants and supporting his colleagues, as well as doing demos and connecting with his fans at local events.

Upcoming ventures from Tom Douglas Restaurants: A rustic Italian restaurant by the name of Couco with an open pasta making station; Bravehorse Tavern, casual dining that will feature burgers, a pretzel oven, and 24 beers on tap; and Ting Momo, focusing on handmade Tibetan dumplings.

See Chef Tom Douglas's recipe for **Jackie's Tomatoes with Avocado Skordalia** on p. 190.

toppings. Thai Curry Simple is open for lunch daily until 3:30 p.m., except Sun. Also see **Thai Curry Simple 2,** p. 83.

Tilikum Place Cafe, 407 Cedar St., Seattle, WA 98121; (206) 282-4830; Belltown; www.tilikumplacecafe.com; $$. This hidden gem is located in a somewhat unexpected location (just off 5th and Denny). The atmosphere is warm, inviting, and as formal as you want it to be, so inviting that you could easily view it as either your morning brunch stop or the perfect spot for a special occasion dinner. Chef Ba Culbert puts all her passion into this food, using seasonal wholesome ingredients executed with a generous hand of life's most precious spice: love. You will find items like pan-seared chicken; country-style pâté; and hand-cut pasta with sage, toasted hazelnuts, and Parmesan. For weekend brunch go straight for the Dutch babies, which come either sweet or savory, or the Tilikum Fry Up: eggs, bacon, beans, tomato, and homemade sausage.

Urbane, 1639 8th Ave.; Seattle, WA 98101; (206) 676-4600; Downtown; www.urbaneseattle.com; $$$. This chic and lively restaurant is located at the Hyatt at Olive 8 hotel at the heart of downtown. It offers an eclectic menu of Northwest fare with rotating menus that reflect the seasonality of key ingredients blended with global inspiration. Choose between the spacious contemporary dining room or a seat at the popular bar. Urbane commissioned Meyer Wells, a local Seattle company, to create its elegant communal table entirely from locally salvaged wood, and the kitchen participates in composting and oil-recycling programs. A Natura water system, which filters city water three additional times and allows for both still and sparkling water, eliminates the need for bottled water at Urbane. Some recommended items are the bacon macaroni and cheese with Beecher's cheese, the charcuterie plate, and pistachio-crusted trout. Be sure not to miss the extensive daily happy hour menu. Last but not least, I hesitate to share my secret retreat, **Elaia,** an eco-friendly and luxurious spa just upstairs from the restaurant. Any spa treatment will get you a pass into the swimming pool and hot tub, a place that provides warmth on even the chilliest winter day.

Zoë, 2137 2nd Ave., Seattle, WA 98121; (206) 256-2060; Belltown; www.restaurantzoe.com; $$$. Located in the heart of Belltown, this restaurant has a classy bistro feel, large windows, and a lively atmosphere. Owned by Scott and Heather Staples (also from **Quinn's**, p. 80), Zoë is where you get sassy comfort food from the best local and seasonal ingredients, with items like crispy-skin chicken breast, summer squash, bacon lardon, date puree, and whole grain mustard jus, or Thundering Hooves braised beef with marinated heirloom tomato salad, roasted Idaho potato, and chèvre.

Andaluca, 407 Olive Way, Seattle, WA 98101; (206) 382-6999; Downtown; www.andaluca.com; $$$. Attached to the Mayflower Hotel in the heart of downtown Seattle, this eatery allows you to experience the warmth of the Mediterranean with lots of romance and enchantment. Comfy booths give you the privacy for those intimate conversations. Andaluca opened in 1996 and is currently under the direction of Chef Wayne Johnson, an outgoing chef who spends much of his free time giving back to the community and participating in local fund-raisers and events. Open for breakfast, lunch, and dinner daily, the menu consists of items like crispy duck cakes, paella, and a vast selection of *pintxos,* small bites of finger food. Andaluca also serves an extensive gluten-free menu with over 20 items to choose from. In the summer, don't miss the refreshing gazpacho.

Chez Shea, 94 Pike St., Suite 34, Seattle, WA 98101; (206) 467-9990; Pike Place Market; www.chezshea.com; $$. Romance is on the menu at this intimate restaurant that has been around for over 28 years. Breathtaking views from the crisp, clean dining room overlook Elliot Bay and Pike Place. The food is primarily French with a touch of Japanese influence. Diners can choose a formal menu, a 7-course tasting menu for $75, or dine from the more casually priced lounge menu. The happy hour is from 4:30 to 6 p.m. in the lounge and bar area, and wines on the menu are either Northwest or French. Recommended: seared *foie gras,* executed differently in each season. In the summer, try the Heirloom Tomato Napoleon, a marriage of heirloom tomatoes, Beecher's cheese curds, arugula, sherried red onions, Trampetti Olive Oil, and sea salt.

Dahlia Lounge, 2001 4th Ave., Seattle, WA 98121; (206) 682-4142; Belltown; tomdouglas.com/index.php/restaurants/dahlia-lounge; $$$. This landmark restaurant has dark red walls, Chinese hanging lanterns, an open kitchen, and an apple-wood-burning grill. For over 20 years, Dahlia Lounge has been the place for the ultimate Northwest experience with options like the sea bar sampler, seared Alaskan halibut, or lemon-scallion Dungeness crab cakes.

Elliot's Oyster House, 1201 Alaskan Way, Seattle, WA 98101; (206) 623-4340; Downtown/Waterfront; www.elliottsoysterhouse .com; $$. Want oysters? You found the right place. This iconic 35-year-old restaurant, located on the center of downtown's breathtaking waterfront, is where you get them. Yes, this a tourist destination, but it's the right venue to choose from 30 different kinds of oysters while you sit and overlook the water. Are you an oyster novice? Tell them that you have never had an oyster, and the first one is on them. Little details like the crab service make this place a hoot. And what is crab service? After you finish your crab, they bring you hot lemon water to soak your hands in. Then they give you crackers to rub on your hands to remove the oils from the crab, and finally a warm towel to finish cleaning your hands. Frugal food lovers can go for the progressive happy hour Mon through Fri from

3 to 6 p.m. when oysters on the half shell start at 50 cents and increase by 25 cents an hour until 6 p.m.

Etta's, 2020 Western Ave., Seattle, WA 98121; (206) 443-6000; Pike Place Market; tomdouglas.com/ index.php/restaurants/ettas; $$$. Warm shades of orange, red, and yellow gracing the walls, colorful glass lamps, and a beautiful view of Elliot Bay are the accents of this Northwest seafood restaurant, right next door to **Seatown** (see p. 131). The menu boasts comfort food with items fresh from the market, like Etta's famous Dungeness crab cakes and Etta's Rub with Love wild king salmon. Open for brunch and dinner 7 days a week.

The Georgian, 411 University St., Seattle, WA 98101; (206) 621-7889; Downtown; www.fairmont.com/seattle/GuestServices /Restaurants/TheGeorgian.htm; $$$$. Located in the Fairmont Olympic Hotel, the Georgian is the destination for an elegant dinner in their upscale dining room, with 20-foot Palladian windows, seven different shades of yellow, and two chandeliers that illuminate the room. Chef Gavin Stephenson prepares classic French food with a Northwest flair. In the mornings, families and hotel guests enjoy breakfast; lunch meetings have a more business attitude, and dinner transforms into a romantic experience with votive candles. Food lovers on a budget can swing by for the "express lunch" daily: a $15 lunch that includes soup, salad, sandwich, and dessert. A private area called the Petit can be reserved for parties up to 12. Call and inquire about the Georgian Tea, a traditional English-style tea with a selection of Fairmont loose leaf teas, tea sandwiches, house-made scones, and savories.

Il Terrazzo Carmine, 411 1st Ave. South, Seattle, WA 98104; (206) 467-7797; Pioneer Square; http://ilterrazzocarmine.com; $$$. This restaurant is Italy at its core from the curtains to the glassware to the Tuscan-style decor. After over 26 years, this hidden gem in Pioneer Square remains one of the top Italian restaurants in Seattle. Owner Carmine still walks around the room greeting the customers, and waiters with Italian accents, locals coming here to feel at home, a gorgeous outside patio, *mozzarella di bufala* shipped from Italy, and fresh pasta and seafood all come together like the melody of an Italian love song. It's romantic but lively, fancy but unpretentious, and undoubtedly charming in every sense of the word. Open for weekday lunch and dinner Mon through Sat, it's an ideal place for business meetings, a celebration, or a nice dinner for two. Make sure to start with the antipasto and don't miss one of the warm and hearty homemade pasta dishes.

Maneki, 304 6th Ave. South, Seattle, WA 98104; (206) 622-2631; Chinatown/International District; www.manekirestaurant.com; $$. Close to the heart of many locals, this Japanese sushi restaurant has an inspiring story to tell. Originally established over 100 years

Raising the Bar

For those nights when you can imagine yourself with a cocktail in hand, here are two local favorites.

The best-known bar in Seattle is **The Zig Zag Cafe** (1501 Western Ave., Suite 202, Seattle, WA 98101; 206-625-1146; www.zigzagseattle .com)—not a "lounge," but a classic cocktail bar on the Pike Street Hill climb between Western (below the Pike Place Market) and the Seattle Aquarium.

This local favorite was named the number one bar in America by *GQ* magazine and Murray Stenson, the lead barman, was named "Best Bartender in America" by his peers at the Tales of the Cocktail festival. Murray A.K.A. "Murr the Blur" is swift, focused, detailed, and personable with a polished barmanship and photographic memory that matches no other. Full menu, because, why not? They've got a captive audience, and the munchies are known to strike even the most hard-bitten cocktail hound. The tiny kitchen sources fresh ingredients from the Market, just up (and up and up) the stairs.

Should you find yourself in Belltown when thirst strikes, head for **Rob Roy** (2332 2nd Ave., Seattle, WA 98121; 206-956-8423; www.robroyseattle.com). Anu Apte bought this comfy lounge—dark leather bar stools, three long shelves of liquors—and with the creative partnership of Zane Harris, they have built a following simply by making outstanding drinks.

You know how most bars just shovel ice cubes into the shaker? Well, Harris grabs a block of ice the size of a brick and chips it with a hammer until it's the perfect shape for your drink, one giant ice cube with the ideal ratio of chilling surface to drink volume. There's also a short menu of bar snacks, including deviled eggs, meat loaf sliders, and mac and cheese. On Analog Tuesday, bring in old records for them to play—nostalgic moments indeed. The lighting may be dim, but the spirits are decidedly bright.

ago in a different location, it served 500-plus customers on the weekends until the beginning of World War II. During the war, the Japanese people were interned in camps, and Maneki was destroyed. In 1946 Maneki was reborn in the space where the internees stored their belongings during the war. Today it still has a loyal following of people coming to dine in the homey, comfortable, and casual atmosphere. Maneki features tatami rooms, Japanese private rooms for groups of 4 to 10, as well as the Hannya lounge with its full bar. For reservations, call and leave a message and someone will call you back to confirm; tatami rooms require a reservation about a week in advance.

Matt's in the Market, 94 Pike St., Suite 32, Seattle, WA 98101; (206) 467-7909; Pike Place Market; www.mattsinthemarket .com; $$$. Take the stairs up to the third floor of the corner building to reveal a hip restaurant with a fish-tank view of the colorful market and its surroundings, a vibrant buzz of an atmosphere and comfort food made with fresh local ingredients. It's an ideal spot for lunch after a trek through the market, an informal first date, or just a nice place to snag a spot on the bar and chat with the locals. Lunch prices are a worthy deal. Recommended: Try the pork belly confit *bahn mi* or Don & Joe's Lamb Burger. **Note:** There is no elevator, so it is not wheelchair accessible.

Metropolitan Grill, 820 2nd Ave., Seattle, WA 98104; (206) 624-3287; Downtown; www.themetropolitangrill.com; $$$$. For those hunger pangs that only a steak will satisfy, dine at a world-

class local steak house. It's not about the
decor, it's the impeccable service, quality
of the meat, generous portions, and
extensive wine list that really make
the Met stand out. Each table is
graced with knowledgeable staff to
help sort through the overwhelming list
of options. As with anything in life, this luxury comes with a
high price tag, making it an ideal destination for events, special
occasions, or business meetings (especially when someone else is
picking up the tab). Daily lunch specials allow diners to eat a hefty
meal that will get them through the day, with options under $20.
Recommended Dessert: hot apple pie, made right in front of your
eyes; watch them brown the apples in butter, brown sugar, and
then light it on fire.

Palace Kitchen, 2030 5th Ave., Seattle, WA 98121; (206) 448-
2001; Belltown; http://tomdouglas.com/index.php/restaurants/
palace-kitchen; $$$. (Just as much a bar as a restaurant, Palace
Kitchen is as happening as can be. Italian chandeliers, velvet
drapes, and a large horseshoe bar are the backdrop for this sultry
but hip local hangout. Lush but homey, you will find classic comfort
food with items like the Palace Burger Royale (wood-grilled Oregon
Country Beef, Dahlia Bakery bun, pickled green tomato, and fries)
and a Double R Ranch New York strip, straight off the grill. Late
night happy hour is the place to be. Check listings for hours.

Road Trip!

A hop, skip, and a ferry ride away from bustling downtown Seattle is quaint and idyllic Bainbridge Island. A short walk from the ferry is where you can find locals sharing coffee and pastries at the beloved **Blackbird Bakery** (210 Winslow Way E., Bainbridge Island, WA 98110; 206-780-1322) in intimate downtown Bainbridge. **Mora Ice Creamery** (139 Madrone Lane, Bainbridge Island, WA 98110; 206-855-1112; www.moraicecream.com), offers ice cream created locally on the island. Try traditional and eclectic flavors made from organic ingredients.

For lunch, consider **Shima Express** (110 Madison Ave. North, Bainbridge Island, WA 98110; 206-780-7768; $), which offers quick and delicious Japanese meals like ramen, teriyaki chicken, and other menu options at $5.99. Next door is **Shima Garden** (112 Madison Ave. North, Bainbridge Island, WA 98110; 206-855-9400; www.shimasushi.com; $$), where you can go for a traditional sushi dinner. Additional dinner options include the charming **Four Swallows Restaurant** (481 Madison Ave. North, Bainbridge Island, WA 98110; 206-842-3397; www.fourswallows.com; $$$) located in a farmhouse dating

Pike Pub & Brewery, 1415 1st Ave., Seattle, WA 98101; (206) 622-6044; Pike Place Market; www.pikebrewing.com; $$. If you run into someone wearing a bow tie and a beer backpack with a beer hose at local events, then you must have crossed paths with Charles Finkel. He and his wife, Rose Ann Finkel, are all about spreading the wealth in the beer world. In 1989, Charles convinced

back to 1889 and offering a menu featuring high-quality Northwest ingredients served with an Italian flair. For a lovely dinner visit **Hitchcock Restaurant** (133 Winslow Way East, Bainbridge Island, WA 98110; 206-201-3789; www .hitchcockrestaurant.com; $$$), which celebrates local farmers with their French-inspired farm-to-table cuisine. Chef and owner Brendan McGill named the restaurant after members of his wife's family who have lived on the island for five generations. The menu changes daily depending on the supply of produce hand delivered from local farms. Hitchcock is located a short walk from the ferry, easily accessible to visitors coming from downtown Seattle.

If you have a car, visit the popular **Bay Hay and Feed Nursery** (10355 N.E. Valley Rd., Bainbridge Island, WA 98110; 206-842-2813) for your gardening needs, and the **Bloedel Reserve** (7571 N.E. Dolphin Dr., Bainbridge Island, WA 98110; 206-842-7631; www.bloedelreserve .org), voted by *USA Today* as one of the 10 greatest botanic gardens in the United States. Don't forget to take a scenic walk along the waterfront before catching the next ferry back to Seattle.

the owner of Liberty Malt Supply Company that Seattle needed a craft brewery to show home brewers how to make good beer. Since then, it has become a tourist spot for A-to-Z beer education. Pike Place Brewery offers its Pike Beer Experience, a $10, 1½-hour tour that will take you through the history of beer and brewing. It ends with a 6-beer Pike Sampler. You wouldn't expect such a

spacious brewery and restaurant to have
the capacity to focus on local, organic,
and sustainable food, but they are able
to pull it off. A hearty menu and private
rooms make this a neat option for groups or
large parties in a sports-bar, pub-type atmosphere. One of the event rooms, the Pike
Museum Room, includes the history of beer.

The Pink Door, 1919 Post Alley, Seattle, WA 98101; (206)
443-3241; Pike Place Market; www.thepinkdoor.net; $$$. Romantic
restaurants are plentiful in Seattle but sometimes life calls for some
spunk. This restaurant started in 1981 as an underground restau-
rant, with no sign, as a place where artists could get together.
Today it is a Seattle institution where Italian-American food meets
swanky and provocative free entertainment from live bands to
cabaret and a $15 Saturday burlesque evening. Finding this place is
tricky but ask any of the vendors in the Pike Place Market and they
will guide you. The menu is very much produce-driven with lots of
vegetables from the market.

Place Pigalle, 81 Pike St., Seattle, WA 98101; (206) 624-
1756; Pike Place Market; www.placepigalle-seattle.com; $$$. There
is something endearing about a restaurant that hasn't changed any
of the decor since 1979; it's charming, the view is breathtaking, and
the French fare showcases the timeless simplicity and abundance
of the Northwest. Find this restaurant concealed behind the fish

throwers in the **Pike Place Fish Market** (see p. 119). Order the mussels or the roasted beet salad with goat cheese.

Shiro's, 2401 2nd Ave., Seattle, WA 98121; (206) 443-9844; Belltown; www.shiros.com; $$$. Chef Shiro Kashiba has become a culinary icon, with two James Beard Awards and a strong Seattle following since 1967, renowned for his classical Japanese technique combined with the best Northwest ingredients. Locals know of Shiro's close relationships with the best seafood suppliers. This is an ideal place to order *omakase,* where the chef will decide what to send out. Other options are full dinner menus where you get salad, soup, or rice with your sushi. Dine at this landmark restaurant and enjoy the traditional old-school atmosphere.

South

A 15-minute drive south from the skyscrapers of downtown takes you to cozy neighborhoods where you'll hear many different languages. You'll feel right at home in the intimate eateries, where friendly owners of ethnic restaurants greet you like a regular, introducing you to foods from worlds far away. Historic Columbia City offers a bustling, diverse neighborhood of family homes, with everything from bakeries to breakfast spots and pizza parlors with lines out the doors. In Georgetown, explore the character of an industrial area that has become an artist's mecca and spend an evening with new friends in a unique communal farm-to-table dining experience.

This chapter includes Beacon Hill, Columbia City, Georgetown, Rainier Beach, Seward Park, and SoDo.

Borracchini's Bakery, 2307 Rainier Ave. South, Seattle, WA 98144; (206) 325-1550; Beacon Hill; www.nowcake.com. This old-fashioned Italian bakery was founded in 1922. They have a large selection of down-home pastries including doughnuts, fried croissants, elephant ears, pies, and more. They also have a full-service deli with sandwiches and panini and a huge selection of breads baked fresh daily. Do you need a cake decorated? They will do it as you wait. You will also find a section of imported Italian foods such as cookies, oils, and other products often found at specialty food shops.

Columbia City Bakery, 4865 Rainier Ave. South, Seattle, WA 98118; (206) 723-6023; Columbia City; www.columbiacitybakery .com. How far would you go for a really good baguette? I am not asking you to walk, but a short drive from downtown will take you to this delicious bread bakery that has made a name for itself. The other favorite here is the *pain de campagne,* a slightly tangy country bread made of whole wheat and rye. Other baked goods include croissants, bear claws, pistachio snails—and the list goes on. They also have a selection of sandwiches and rich, savory items like quiches and pretzel dogs. If you stop by in the evening, pop in a few doors down for dinner at **La Medusa** (see p. 162), a Sicilian restaurant by the same owners, Evan and Julie Andres. Recommended: the fruit Danish topped with generous amounts of fruit and cream cheese. Do you want to support your carb habit while really connecting with the bakers? Join the CSB, a community supported bakery, where you purchase a 6-week membership and receive the baked goods at a pick-up location near you.

Delite Bakery, 2701 15th Ave. South, Seattle, WA 98144; (206) 325-2114; Beacon Hill. Seekers of *pan de sal,* the fluffy traditional Filipino bread rolls, will find gold at this authentic Filipino bakery with items like *pan de leche, turrón* (banana and jackfruit spring rolls), *karioka* (chewy rice balls on a stick), *pandan* cakes, *ube* (purple yam) cakes, *ensaïmadas,* and more. Pastry lovers will enjoy the unique selection, and this is a nice, inexpensive option for special-occasion sheet cakes. I love their version of *babingka,* a coconut and cheese cake. They are closed on Sunday. The low prices and surprising selection make this bakery a true gem.

The Essential Baking Company, 5601 1st Ave. South, Seattle, WA 98108; (206) 876-3746; Georgetown; www.essentialbaking.com. For a full description see the North listing, p. 5.

Full Tilt, 5041 Rainier Ave. South, Seattle, WA 98118; (206) 226-2740; Columbia City; www.fulltilticecream.com. (See website for additional locations.) Give an adult an ice-cream cone and watch them turn back 20 years; give that same adult a room full of vintage arcade games and pinball machines and the rest is history. Meet Full

Tilt, where you can play arcade games while you eat fresh artisan ice cream in fun and original flavors like coffee Oreo, chocolate ginger, lemon lavender, salted licorice, mango, and chili. Both Columbia City and White Center locations serve beer and hold live music events. Check the website for listings.

Macrina, 1943 1st Ave. South, Seattle, WA 98134; (206) 623-0919; SoDo; www.macrinabakery.com. For a full description see the Downtown listing, p. 103.

Oberto Sausage, 1715 Rainier Ave. South, Seattle, WA 98144; (206) 322-7524; Beacon Hill; www.obertosausagecompany.com. If snacking on salty strips of meat is your guilty pleasure, then this Oberto factory outlet store is where you can get your beef jerky fix. Nothing fancy here but racks and racks of beef jerky, sausages, and other Oberto-brand products at cheap prices.

Specialty Stores & Markets

Big John's PFI, 1001 6th Ave. South, Level B, Seattle, WA 98134; (206) 682-2022; SoDo; www.bigjohnspfiseattle.com. Some call this place Big John's, some Pacific Food Importers, but most call it PFI. The titles don't matter when it comes to this being a prized specialty store in Seattle. This unassuming warehouse is where chefs and food lovers swoon over the colossal selection of cheeses, colorful selection of by-the-pound olives, buckets of legumes, and monster-size containers of pasta. They also have a large selection of olive oils, specialty Mediterranean products, and more, at competitive prices. They are closed on Sunday. There is a 1-pound minimum for cheese, olives, and cured meats although half pounds of cheeses can be sold if they cost over $20 a pound. You can also sweet talk your way into a lighter pound. Bring your own container with a tight lid and they will pack your olives in brine. *Note:* Free parking is available in the parking lot.

Bob's Quality Meats, 4861 Rainier Ave. South, Seattle, WA 98118; (206) 725-1221; Columbia City. Since 1909, this butcher shop has been serving the Columbia City area with the highest quality meats. The owner, James (Bob is his father), is one of the most friendly and personable people around. Here you can find the usual meats, house-made items like prosciutto and pancetta, and harder-to-find items like buffalo, elk, venison, and rabbit. They also offer whole animals such as goat, sheep, and pigs on request. Customers will drive across town for Bob's artisan sausages, with over 20 varieties including the popular Cajun boudin and the bratwurst.

Foulee Market & Deli, 2050 S. Columbian Way, Seattle, WA 98108; (206) 764-9607; Beacon Hill. There is nothing more fun than finding a market full of vegetables and herbs that are new to you. This Filipino market has a large selection of Asian vegetables and fruits along with other ethnic finds. You will find at least four varieties of eggplant including Filipino, Chinese, and Indian ones; bitter melon; chayote squash; *kangkong* leaves, and other finds for creative cooks. They also have Asian staples like Filipino breads and imported cookies and some uncommon meat items like pork stomach, pork intestines, and pork blood. In the deli section, they have chicken gizzards, barbecued pork, pork adobo, smelt fish, and other specialties. It is a great place to find inexpensive produce.

Mutual Fish, 2335 Rainier Ave. South, Seattle, WA 98144; (206) 322-4368; Beacon Hill; www.mutualfish.com. If you ask local chefs and restaurateurs where they get their seafood, chances are Mutual Fish will come up in the conversation. Seafood lovers alike swear by the quality, service, and selection of this three-generation-old retail and wholesale company, owned by the Yoshimura family since 1947. Here you can find black cod, sea bass, and other fillets, and a large selection of oysters, mussels, prawns, and sushi-grade fish. Don't miss the live seafood with Manila clams, geo-

duck, Dungeness crab, and more. Overnight shipping available, and it is a kosher approved facility.

Road Trip!

To escape the urban bustle, Seattleites head to Orcas Island for a day or weekend getaway. Orcas Island lies in the heart of the San Juan Island archipelago. Known for its miles of solitude, lush landscape, local farms, wildlife, and quaint coves, it has captivated national attention as a major travel destination. The island is sheltered from the erratic Pacific Northwest storm channel, allowing for more sunny days than the greater Seattle metropolitan area. Showers in western Washington tend to be a good forecaster for clear skies on the island.

The journey to Orcas Island is a beautiful ferry ride, only an hour and a half north of Seattle. Travel to the ferry is packed with adventure: snow-capped mountains, fields of blossoming red tulips, apple farms, and green pastures. Short on time? Take a breathtaking 30-minute floatplane over the islands via Kenmore Air direct from Seattle.

Don't miss **Allium Restaurant** (310 Main St., Orcas Island, WA 98245; 360-376-4904; www.alliumonorcas.com; $$$) run by Chef Lisa Nakamura, formerly of **the Herbfarm** (see p. 109) and the French Laundry (in Napa). The menu changes frequently to keep in stride with the growing season, focusing on clean, bright Pacific Northwest

PCC Natural Markets, 5041 Wilson Ave. South, Seattle, WA 98118; (206) 723-2720; Seward Park; www.pccnaturalmarkets.com. For a full description see the North listing, p. 16.

flavors. Ingredients are sourced from local farms, and signature dishes include polenta with roasted forest mushrooms and sunny-side-up Black Dog Farm duck eggs, Jones Family Farm Manila clams with local saffron aioli, and the daily gnocchi drizzled with truffle oil, which has taken on a cultlike following. Finish with mango cheeescake or chocolate pudding cake and a pot of French press local coffee. Have pets? Don't forget to grab a bag of house-made dog biscuits for the road. Other popular island activities include year-round kayaking, whale watching, and a scenic drive to Mount Constitution, the highest mountain in the entire archipelago (elevation of 2,409 feet). The summit boasts 360-degree views of the 450 islands that make up the San Juan Island chain, including spectacular vistas of the Cascades and Olympic Mountain range.

Rose's Bakery & Cafe (382 Prune Alley, Eastsound, WA 98245; 360-376-5805; Orcas Island) is the perfect stop before taking in the stunning view atop Mount Constitution. Pack a picnic basket with local and organic finds. Choose from a wide variety of cheese, wine, baked goods, sandwiches, soups, and salads. The bakery also features artisan breads, gourmet grocery items, glassware, and chocolate.

Viet Wah Super Foods, 6040 Martin Luther King Jr. Way, Seattle, WA 98118; (206) 760-8895; Columbia City; www.vietwah.com. For a full description see the Downtown listing, p. 122.

The Corson Building, 5609 Corson Ave. South, Seattle, WA 98108; (206) 762-3330; Georgetown; www.thecorsonbuilding.com; $$$$. Surrender to a dining experience. In a beautiful house turned restaurant in the middle of Georgetown, South Seattle's industrial area, there are no menus. You are to leave the entire dinner menu up to Chefs Matt Dillon and Emily Crawford. The multicourse dinner is composed of the best ingredients they can find: a full pig, assorted seafood, or fresh ingredients from the backyard of the Corson Building. Be prepared to make conversation as you'll be randomly seated with those present at dinner. The price is $90, and wine pairings are available on request. This special dinner format is available on Saturday, but during the week you can order a la carte; check the website for availability. A $23 brunch is available on the weekend, as well as a Sunday supper.

El Pilón, 5303 Rainier Ave. South, Seattle, WA 98118; (206) 577-7165; Columbia City; www.elpilonseattle.com; $. You'll probably miss the sign for this little Puerto Rican hole-in-the-wall, but that's okay because owner and mother of the house Marta Vega's warm and welcoming smile will make you feel right at home. Order the mofongo, a round ball of goodness made of mashed plantains and filled with your choice of fried meat, served in a hand-made wooden pilón (mortar and pestle). Pair that with empanadas, and you'll have everything you need. Fruit smoothies and shakes are also great drink options. Don't come in a hurry—this is not that kind of place. Instead, the homey feeling and authentic vibe will make you feel like you're eating in your grandmother's kitchen.

El Quetzal, 3209 Beacon Ave. South, Seattle, WA 98144; (206) 329-2970; Beacon Hill; www.elquetzalseattle.com; $. This small Mexican restaurant, hidden in Beacon Hill, is as homey as it is appetizing with its warm decor of moons all over the wall and the staff who care how you feel about the food. Go for the *huaraches gigantes,* a "sandal shaped" corn dough with refried beans, cheese, lettuce, and sour cream, or the enchiladas verdes with rice, beans, and warm tortillas, or anything else off the extensive and inexpensive menu. Order the Horchata made of rice milk, cinnamon, and vanilla to drink. El Quetzal is kid friendly, great for takeout, and a good value.

Ezell's Famous Chicken, 11805 Renton Ave. South (next to Skyway Bowl), Seattle, WA 98178; (206) 772-1925; Rainier Beach; www.ezellschicken .com. For a full description see the Central listing, p. 70.

Flying Squirrel Pizza, 4920 S. Genesee St., Seattle, WA 98118; (206) 721-7620; Seward Park; www.flyingsquirrelpizza.com; $. (See website for additional locations.) Crowds fill this neighborhood pizza joint for the handmade artisan pizza with toppings by local purveyors like Zoe's Meats and **Salumi Artisan Cured Meats**

A SWEET DRIVE TO KENT

Rumors about **Punjab Sweets** (23617 104th Ave. Southeast C, Kent, WA 98031; 253-859-3236; www.punjabsweetsonline.com; $) circulate freely in the food community, where cravings for Indian desserts drive people to travel to Kent to get their hands on the rows of colorful handmade sweets. This family-owned confectionary and eatery started as a hole-in-the-wall bakery, where Iqbal Dha shared the Indian sweets that she baked for weddings and friends. It wasn't long before Punjab Sweets gained a loyal following and expanded to what is now the current restaurant. Specialties include items like *gulab jamun,* balls of sweet pastry; *jalebi,* a fennel cake dipped in homemade syrup; pistachio *burfi,* fudge made of pure cream and pistachios; and *rasgulla,* doughnut holes made of sweet cheese. Enjoy savory snacks like spicy fried chickpeas and their homemade spicy Indian mix. Punjab Sweets also serves lunch and dinner in Indian *thali* trays filled with different items to taste and dishes like the *maki di roti with saag* (corn flour chapati served with spinach and greens blended to a smooth seasoned paste). All menu items are vegetarian, and many of the items are made without gluten. If the drive is a little far for your taste, rest assured that you can order the sweets and snacks to be delivered anywhere in the United States.

(see p. 104). The texture of the crust is thin, tender and holds up without sogginess. Build your own pizza or choose one of their classics, made with the freshest, high-quality, and organic ingredients when possible. The kid-friendly restaurant plays mix tapes from the '70s, '80s, and '90s. Donate an old mix tape and get 10 percent off your next order.

Geraldine's Counter, 4872 Rainier Ave. South, Seattle, WA 98118; (206) 723-2080; Columbia City; www.geraldinescounter .com; $$. This Columbia City American diner has become a destination breakfast favorite, with families and friends lining out the door for the famous French toast and morning menu. Here you will find items like homemade biscuits and gravy, chicken-fried steak and eggs, omelets, and so many other hearty breakfast treats. They are also open for lunch and dinner—the wholesome homemade food and reasonable prices make this place a great treat any time of day. Come early in the mornings (like 8 a.m.) and you might be able to escape or at least shorten the wait; if there are only two in your party you might be able to snag a spot at the counter. Kids are especially welcome here, with crayons to keep them busy. The owners Gary Snyder and Stacy Hettinger also own Table 219 in Capitol Hill, where you can find fun and original comfort food and an innovative brunch menu.

Hallava Falafel, 5825 Airport Way South, Seattle, WA 98108; (206) 307-4769; Georgetown; http://hallavafalafel.com; $. Don't judge a truck by its cover. This yellow food truck has the most divine falafel and *shawarma* around. Here you can get a falafel or *shawarma* filled with tzatziki made with Armenian cucumbers and Russian Red Relish, a name for their beet salad that the owner made when he noticed that people tend to resist beets, as well as spinach, cabbage, and iceberg lettuce. For vegans they have tahini sauce too. The truck is parked at the same location Tues through Sat, 11 a.m. to 3 p.m.

Kusina Filipina, 3201 Beacon Ave. South, Seattle, WA 98144; (206) 322-9433; Beacon Hill; $. This small-scale restaurant is nothing fancy, but the warmth and flavors of this place will usher you into the world of Filipino food. Grab your food at the counter and take a seat at a table surrounded with Filipino art, books, and ethnic decorations. Don't worry if you are unfamiliar with the foods, the lovely staff is eager to explain. You will find chicken and pork adobo, rich meats cooked in a vinegar-soy sauce, *lumpia* (Filipino egg rolls), and other specialties. This is a great place for a quick lunch of really good value.

La Medusa, 4857 Rainier Ave. South, Seattle, WA 98118; (206) 723-2192; Columbia City; www.lamedusarestaurant.com; $$. Since 1997, La Medusa has been Columbia City's homey Sicilian restaurant with an upbeat atmosphere. The current owners, Julie and Evan Andres, also own **Columbia City Bakery** (see p. 151) and have kept traditional Sicilian food with the same quality and passion, made with seasonal produce from local farmers' markets. Choose from the *piatti della casa* menu, the 3-course market menu, or the chalkboard specials. Families with kids tend to trickle in between

5:30 and 6:30 p.m., and later hours boast a more buzzing atmosphere. Recommended: *perciatelli con le sarde,* sardine sauce on perchiatelli noodles. Most times are busy but Tuesday and Thursday are days to beat the crowd.

Tutta Bella, 4918 Rainier Ave. South, Seattle, WA 98118; (206) 721-3501; Columbia City; (425) 391-6838; www.tuttabella pizza.com; $$. (See website for additional locations.) When you enter a Tutta Bella pizzeria, you'll feel the warmth of the wood-burning ovens and smell the hot Regina Margherita pizza. Founded in 2004 by Joe Fugere, Tutta Bella is the Northwest's first Vera Pizza Napoletana (VPN)–certified Neapolitan pizzeria and is held accountable to high culinary standards. They use only organic San Marzano D.O.P. *(Denominazione d' Origine Protetta)* tomatoes, fresh mozzarella, fresh herbs, and finely ground "00" *(doppio zero)* flour. Attibassi espresso is flown in weekly direct from Italy and prepared at the Neapolitan-style espresso bar. In addition to pizza, menu items include calzones, antipasti, signature salads, soup, house-made desserts, and gelato. Families with kids will love the friendly attitude and the Wikki Stix they give the kids to keep them busy. They also offer kids dough to play with on request.

Via Tribunali, 6009 12th Ave. South, Seattle, WA 98108; (206) 464-2880; Georgetown; www.viatribunali.net; $$. For a full description see the Central listing, p. 84.

West Seattle

When you drive west from downtown and cross the West Seattle bridge, you feel like you're approaching a remote island. The evening sunlight illuminates the downtown Seattle waterfront with a stunning golden glow. This magical route takes you to the beautiful beaches of Alki, where summer concerts fill the streets and breathtaking views of the Olympic Mountains dominate the waterfront. West Seattle is a tight-knit community where residents take pride in neighborhood gems and family-friendly options. Just look at the food. The casual attitude of West Seattleites colors the food establishments, rich in history and character, day or night.

Made Here

Bakery Nouveau, 4737 California Ave. Southwest, Seattle, WA 98116; West Seattle, (206) 923-0534; www.bakerynouveau.com. It doesn't get much better than this. Where shall one start? Start with a croissant, the twice-baked almond croissant to be precise, then move to the baguettes. Now what? Sample Parisian macarons, a slice of their classic chocolate cake, and one of the 30-plus varieties of handmade chocolates. During the week, get pizza by the slice, but on Friday and Saturday come in and pick up a full pizza fresh out of the oven. The masterminds behind one of the top bakeries in town are William and Heather Leaman. As the captain of the 2005 Bread Bakers Guild Team USA, William led his team to victory at the Coupe du Monde de la Boulangerie (World Cup of Baking) and won numerous awards and accomplishments.

Cupcake Royale and Vérité Coffee, 4556 California Ave. Southwest, Seattle, WA 98116; (206) 932-2971; West Seattle; www .cupcakeroyale.com. For a full description see the Central listing, p. 44.

The Original Bakery, 9253 45th Ave. Southwest, Seattle, WA 98109; (206) 938-5088; West Seattle. Since 1974, this family-owned bakery has been making their signature cake doughnuts with all-natural ingredients throughout the day. Some favorites are the maple bars and apple fritters. They also make fresh Danishes, pastries, cookies, and various fresh breads. Check out the bread of the day. Once you have chosen your favorite, the trick is to call in and ask them to reserve your chosen flavor. The bakery is closed Mon and open Tues through Fri 7 a.m. to 6 p.m.; Sat 7 a.m. to 5 p.m.; and Sun 8 a.m. to 3 p.m.

Shoofly Pie Company, 4444 California Ave. Southwest, Seattle, WA 98116; (206) 938-0680; West Seattle; www.shooflypiecompany .com. We all need a little pie in our life. For this, Shoofly really hits the spot. They have a selection of pies like banana cream, chocolate cream, and seasonal fruit pies, and savory pies like veggie, beef, and chicken potpies. They start to sell and slice more pies closer to the weekend so your best bet for selection would be from Thursday onward. And for those who want a bit of everything, order the smaller-size cup pies and cutie pies, and mix and match. The quaint seating area is a nice place for an afternoon read with your pie.

Sugar Rush Baking Company, 4541 California Ave. Southwest, Seattle, WA 98116; (206) 937-1495; West Seattle; www.sugarrush bakingcompany.com. Also known as Coffee to Tea with Sugar, this voluminous bakery cafe has everything you want in a neighborhood hangout: an upbeat, family-friendly atmosphere, board games, and a toy-rich kids area in the back of the room that gives the parents some time to chat and the kids some freedom to play. Those without kids can sit on the other side of the bakery to avoid the hustle. Cupcakes take the cake here, with minis and originals in so many flavors, frosted sugar cookies, rugelach, and tasty Key lime bars. Miniature 99-cent bags of sprinkles will give your kids the cupcake-decorating edge, and for sweet occasions, create your own cake; choosing the frosting, filling, and base. See the **Sugar Rush Baking Company Scones** recipe on p. 212.

Specialty Stores & Markets

Husky Deli & Catering, 4721 California Ave. Southwest, Seattle, WA 98116; (206) 937-2810; West Seattle; www.huskydeli.com. It is all about the ice cream. Walk down California Avenue Southwest and you will see people clutching their cones. You don't even have to ask where they got them because the West Seattle residents agree that Husky Deli is where you go for hand-crafted ice cream in all the flavors from basic banana to caramel pecan fudge. But it is not only about the ice cream, they have wonderful deli sandwiches, a generous selection of candy, and other grocery selections you may need. This iconic deli and specialty shop has been satisfying cravings since 1932, so come broaden your food horizons and indulge in a great meal, with your ice cream of course.

Metropolitan Market, 2320 42nd Ave. Southwest, Seattle, WA 98116; (206) 937-0551; West Seattle; www.metropolitan-market .com. For a full description see the Central listing, p. 59.

PCC Natural Markets, 2749 California Ave. Southwest, Seattle, WA 98116; (206) 937-8481; West Seattle; www.pccnaturalmarkets .com. For a full description see the North listing, p. 16.

Seattle Fish Company, 4435 California Ave. Southwest, Seattle, WA 98116; (206) 938-7576; West Seattle; www.seattlefishcompany .com. While driving down California Avenue Southwest, you might notice the signs in the window for different kinds of fish. This specialty fish store focuses on quality, freshness and local fish. You can find a large selection of seafood from halibut and salmon to all kinds of prawns and shellfish, sashimi grade fish and house-smoked fish. Their daily shipment assures that your fish arrives fresh. Seattle Fish also has wines and a knowledgeable staff who can help pair wines and sauces with your seafood meal. Recommended: any of the house-smoked fish, especially the black cod or the salmon, and the house-made crab cakes. Order online and they will ship to anywhere in the United States.

The Swinery, 3207 California Ave. Southwest, Seattle, WA 98116; (206) 932-4211; West Seattle; www.theswinery.blogspot.com. Homer Simpson's quote, "Porkchops and bacon, my two favorite animals," would be a great slogan for this deli counter full of everything pork: belly, trotters, cheeks, smoked ham, and house-made apple-wood smoked bacon. The Swinery promotes small, local, sustainable farms, butchering everything from whole animals in-house, including beef and poultry. The lunch menu rotates daily with options like the Swinery Burger made of Thundering Hooves ground beef on a brioche bun with caramelized onions. There is a tiny seating area inside and a courtyard for outdoor seating. Don't forget to pick up some bacon caramels or bacon–chocolate chip cookies by Sugar & Salt Kitchen.

Food Lovers' Faves

Blackboard Bistro, 3247 California Ave. Southwest, Seattle, WA 98116; (206) 257-4832; West Seattle; http://blackboardbistro seattle.com; $$. The writing is on the wall, or blackboards, to be precise. No menus in sight, it's all about what's fresh and seasonal. Chef Jacob Wiegner offers new and varietal dishes, incorporating nostalgic dishes from his nomadic past, having traveled to New Zealand, Australia, England, and places in the United States. It is a laid-back bistro where comfort food meets classy French technique. Families with kids can order off the 3-course children's tasting menu, and the best way to go, for the fully grown, is the name-your-price tasting menu: Any price will do, and the chef will send out his favorites that night.

Buddha Ruksa, 3520 S.W. Genesee St., Seattle, WA 98126; West Seattle; (206) 937-7676; www.buddharuksa.com; $. This popular Thai restaurant has become a destination for devoted food lovers looking for their Thai fix. The relaxing and calming atmosphere, authentic offerings of the standard Thai classics and friendly service makes for a West Seattle gem. Recommended: the appetizer sampler platter or the Bags of Gold and the must-have crispy garlic chicken. No MSG is used, and vegetarians will find a large selection of tofu options.

Circa Neighborhood Grill and Alehouse, 2605 California Ave. Southwest, Seattle, WA; 98116; (206) 923-1102; West Seattle; www .circawestseattle.com; $$. If you live in West Seattle, you'll probably run into your neighbors who often frequent this place. This alehouse has creative comfort menu items like the juicy Circa Burger or duck leg confit with gingered sweet potato puree and orange marmalade. Those wanting lighter bar snacks can get any of the small-plate items, like the crispy sweet potato fries. A popular brunch item is the Big and Fluffy Banana Pancakes. This family-friendly establishment serves top-notch food with high quality ingredients in a casual atmosphere. Recommended: grilled steak salad.

Ephesus of Seattle, 5245 California Ave. Southwest, Seattle, WA 98136; (206) 937-3302; West Seattle; www.ephesusseattle.com; $$. This Turkish restaurant located in a renovated house is a nice place to find warmth on a chilly day. I bet pita is not on your list of comfort foods, but one bite of this puffy, warm, house-made flat bread and you will be revising that list. Hummus is to pita what butter is to bread, so start your order with hummus or the assortment plate of dips and taste to your heart's content. They are known for their kebabs, which come in a selection of meats. I recommend the juicy Adana kebab made with ground lamb. This is also great choice for takeout.

Fresh Bistro, 4725 42nd Ave. Southwest, Seattle, WA 98116; (206) 935-3733; West Seattle; www.freshbistroseattle.com; $$. This farm-to-table bistro features seasonally inspired Pacific Northwest cuisine in a welcoming atmosphere with indoor and outdoor seating. Open for lunch on weekdays, brunch on weekends, and dinner 7 days a week. The family-style options are a great way to share: a seafood-boil dinner for 4 at $25 dollars a person includes scallops, clams, prawns, mussels, crab, and andouille sausage paired with a salad, truffle-honey corn bread, and a dessert. Reservations required for this option. Check the website for happy hour, when you can order the Herban Bento, a selection of 6 bites from the menu for $25. Recommended menu items: braised pork belly *banh mi* sandwich or the Wagyu-Lamb Burger.

Jak's Grill, 4548 California Ave. Southwest, Seattle, WA 98116; West Seattle; (206) 937-7809; www .jaksgrill.com; $$$. (See website for additional locations.) This local neighborhood chain gets the steak house thing right, straight and simple. The aged corn-fed Nebraska-raised beef is dry or wet aged for a minimum of 28 days and comes with generous sides at dinner time like the humongous baked potato and

lots of vegetables. And who doesn't like a morning brunch happy hour with items for $5 from 9 to 10 a.m., Saturday and Sunday? They don't take reservations, so be prepared to wait in line. All in all, it's all about the value here, and though it may be not fancy shmancy, it totally fits the bill.

La Rustica, 4100 Beach Dr. SW, Seattle, WA 98116; (206) 932-3020; West Seattle; www.larusticarestaurant.com; $$$. West Seattle residents are infatuated with Janie and Giulio Pellegrini's Italian hideaway and it's old-world, classic atmosphere. As quaint as it is busy, this treasure trove is where central Italian food meets a loving neighborhood hangout. Find menu items like Cioppino allo Zafferano (mussels, clams, calamari, scallops, prawns, and salmon in a spicy saffron broth) or Lasagna di Nonna Marcella (lasagna noodles layered with a Bolognese sauce, mushrooms, eggs, peas, and mozzarella cheese). Many of the pastas—such as the ravioli, tortellini, lasagna, and gnocchi—are made by hand. They don't take reservations for parties under 6, so avoid waits by coming in either early or later during the evening. Ask about the neighborhood's adopted favorite dish, the roasted lamb shanks in a balsamic reduction.

Mashiko, 4725 California Ave. Southwest, Seattle, WA 98116; (206) 935-4339; West Seattle; www.sushiwhore.com; $$. You gotta love a restaurant that uses the web address "sushi whore." It's not your conventional sushi spot, but telling by how busy it gets, you know it's a favorite. Sushi Chef Hajime Sato has a sense of humor but he has rules: Soy sauce is not a beverage, and chopsticks are not drumsticks, and because Hajime said so, a complete list can be found on the website under "think" (and then proceed to "obey"). Don't let his playful attitude fool you—this place is serious about their sushi. So serious, in fact, that in August 2009, after celebrating 15 years of business, Mashiko became Seattle's first fully sustainable sushi restaurant, using only fish caught and farmed responsibly, with minimal bycatch and no antibiotics. In addition to sushi, they have *izakaya* items, bento, tempura, curry, and more. Wondering who is sitting at the bar? Follow the website webcam and take a look!

Phonecia, 2716 Alki Ave. Southwest, Seattle, WA 98116; (206) 935-6550; West Seattle; www.phoeneciawestseattle.com; $$. If I could choose a restaurant just based on ambience alone, this spot would top the charts. The location, across from Alki Beach, is a warm bistro with its candlelit dining and a sexy bar that makes it an inviting and romantic spot for a date, dinner with friends, or a quick evening bite. It is a neighborhood bistro, offering small plates and tapas with local ingredients. Until not too long ago, this was a Lebanese restaurant run by Hussein Khazaal, who charmed the world with his generous will-cook-for-you-attitude; after he passed away unexpectedly, his kin decided to bring back the beloved restaurant with a modern twist. You can still find little touches of Lebanese in the food, and as the food is still taking shape, one cannot miss the quality that Hussein passed on to his family, a warm, genuine hospitality very characteristic of the Lebanese culture—truly a place for some wine and a meal with friends.

Spring Hill, 4437 California Ave. Southwest, Seattle, WA 98116; (206) 935-1075; West Seattle; www.springhillnorthwest.com. $$$. Sophisticated and contemporary Spring Hill is a creative playground for Chef Mark Fuller; he uses local and seasonal ingredients for his creations. So local, in fact, that you can find the names of the farms on the menu. Find house-made charcuterie and pasta, adventurous plays on local seafood, and yes, a restaurant open on Monday nights. Having trouble deciding what to order? Opt for the $38 prix fixe. Want to impress your food lovin' date? Ask for the table for two with the view of the kitchen. This is the place to go for weekend brunch or if you are dining on a dime catch the happy hour in the bar area Tues through Fri from 5:45 to 7 p.m. For a taste of the Northwest, order the Geoduck (pronounced "gooey duck"), a king clam that they source from local favorite, Taylor Shellfish Farms. See Chef Mark Fuller's recipe for **Apple Wood Grilled Spot Prawns** on p. 198.

The Tuscan Tea Room, 4521 California Ave. Southwest, Seattle, WA 98116; (206) 906-9914; West Seattle; www.thetuscantearoom .com; $$. Our busy, fast-paced lives may keep us from taking time to breathe, but tea in the afternoon is a reminder that snacks don't have to be chips at the desk. Come into this elegant tearoom and order from one of the tea menus and an assortment of Tuscan nibbles such as the *tramezzini* (mini tea sandwiches), bruschetta, quiche, and items like cheese, prosciutto di Parma, and seasonal fruit. Owner Aimee Pelligrini inherited her love of food from her parents, the lovely owners of **La Rustica** (see p. 172), and merged her love of flowers into this eatery and flower shop. Intricate decor, gold accents, and antique embellishments create an upscale and beautiful atmosphere, the perfect space to enjoy a selection of over 65 different teas. Children will love playing grown-up and ordering the Tea for Tots tasting menu.

Landmark Eateries

Luna Park Cafe, 2918 S.W. Avalon Way, Seattle, WA 98126; (206) 935-7250; West Seattle; www.lunaparkcafe.com; $. Dubbed the Coney Island of the West, Luna Park was actually an amusement park from 1907 to 1913 with a merry-go-round, a figure-eight roller coaster, and a cluster of amusement rides. The park closed in 1913, leaving only a saltwater natatorium, which was torched by an arsonist in 1931. After World War II, different taverns were established in this space until 1989, when the Luna Park Cafe opened its doors, paying tribute to times past with mismatched signs and images, jukeboxes, comfy booths, and a rocking Batmobile in the corner of the room. This kid-friendly diner is where you'll find generous breakfast items all day long, sandwiches, burgers, and old fashioned milk shakes, a must have with any order. Other neighborhood favorites are the Elvis burger made with cheddar cheese, bacon, and peanut butter and the Elvis waffle with peanut butter, banana, and bacon.

Salty's on Alki Beach, 1936 Harbor Ave. Southwest, Seattle, WA 98126; (206) 937-1600; West Seattle; and **Salty's at Redondo Beach,** 28201 Redondo Beach Dr. South, Des Moines, WA 98198; (253) 946-0636; Des Moines; www.saltys.com; $$$. This is the place you want to take out-of-town guests looking for a view. Surrounded by water, with floor-to-ceiling windows that look out to a view of the Seattle skyline across Elliott Bay, Salty's is a landmark restaurant and home of many Seattle memories. At Salty's you can find Northwest seafood for breakfast, lunch, and dinner. Buffet lovers and people with hungry kids to feed will find solace in the weekend buffet: all-you-can-eat Dungeness crab, fresh local oysters, clams, sausage, bacon and ham, a pasta bar, omelets, Belgian waffles, house-made baked items, and a build-your-own Bloody Mary bar. This is one of three large waterfront restaurants, the others on Redondo Beach and in Portland, Oregon. Salty's is the destination to win you endless show-off points with tourists.

Farm Fresh

Seattle is lucky to have farmers' markets in many neighborhoods, bringing together farmers, local producers of artisanal goods, and food lovers. Here are some of the local markets in the Seattle area. Many of the farmers' markets are part of the Neighborhood Farmers Market Alliance (NFMA), www.seattlefarmersmarkets.org. Farmers' market days and hours may change periodically, so please check the websites for more details. Note that some of these markets are also flea markets and sell more than just food.

Ballard Farmers' Market, located at Ballard Avenue Northwest, between Vernon Place Northwest and 22nd Avenue Northwest, Seattle, WA 98107; www.myballard.com/ballard-sunday-farmers -market. Sun 10 a.m. to 3 p.m., year-round, rain, snow, sun, and/ or wind.

Broadway Sunday Farmers' Market, located at 10th Ave E. and E. Thomas St., Seattle, WA, 98102 (entrances are on Broadway, Thomas, and 10th Avenue E.); www.seattlefarmersmarkets.org/markets/broadway. Sun 11 a.m. to 3 p.m., May through Dec.

Cascade Farmers' Market, South Lake Union's Farmers' Market located on Minor Avenue between Thomas and Harrison Streets, 2 blocks west of REI; www.cascadefarmersmarket.org. Thurs 3 to 7 p.m.

Columbia City Farmers' Market, Edmunds Street between 37th and the alley at 36th (just off Rainier in the heart of Columbia City); www.seattlefarmersmarkets.org/markets/columbiacity. Wed 3 to 7 p.m., Apr through Oct.

Fremont Market, 3401 Evanston Ave. North, Seattle, WA 98103; www.fremontmarket.com. Sun 10 a.m. to 5 p.m., rain or shine.

Georgetown Farmers' Markets, Original Rainier Brewery, 6000 Airport Way South in the Georgetown District between the General Offices building and the old Malt House; http://georgetownfarmers market.wordpress.com. Sat 10 a.m. to 3 p.m., June to Oct.

Lake City Farmers' Market, located next to the Library at N.E. 125th and 28th Avenue Northeast, Seattle, WA 98125; www.seattlefarmersmarkets.org/markets/lake_city. Thurs 3 to 7 p.m., June through Oct.

Madrona Farmers' Market, located in the parking lot of the Madrona Grocery Outlet at the corner of Martin Luther King Jr.

Way and E. Union Street, Seattle, WA 98122; www.madronafarmers market.wordpress.com. Fri 3 to 7 p.m., May through Sept.

Magnolia Farmers' Market, located next to the Magnolia Community Center at 2550 34th Ave. West, Seattle, WA 98199; www.seattlefarmersmarkets.org/markets/magnolia. Sat 10 a.m. to 2 p.m., June through Sept.

Phinney Farmers' Markets, in the lower parking lot at the Phinney Neighborhood Center, 67th and Phinney Avenue North, Seattle, WA 98103; www.seattlefarmers markets.org/markets/phinney. Fri 3 to 7 p.m., May through Oct.

Pike Place Market, open year-round. For a description, see pages 92 to 93 of the Downtown chapter.

Queen Anne Farmers' Market, W. Crockett Street at Queen Anne Avenue North, Seattle WA 98109; www.qafma.org. Thurs 4 to 8 p.m., June through Sept.

University District Farmers' Market, University Way and N.E. 50th Avenue, Seattle, WA 98105; on the playlot of the University Heights Center for the Community; www.seattlefarmersmarkets.org/markets/udistrict. Sat 9 a.m. to 2 p.m., year-round.

Wallingford Farmers' Market, the corner of Wallingford Avenue North and N. 45th Street, Seattle, WA 98116; www.wallingford farmersmarket.wordpress.com. Wed 3 to 7 p.m., May through Sept.

West Seattle Farmers' Market, located at 44th Avenue Southwest and S.W. Alaska Street, Seattle, WA 98116; www.seattle farmersmarkets.org/markets/westSeattle. Sun 10 a.m. to 2 p.m., year-round.

Culinary Instruction

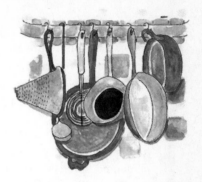

Cooking classes are a fun way to make new friends, inspire you in the kitchen, and introduce yourself to new techniques and ingredients. It's a great way to break the ice on a first date or just an interactive way to get the people you love together.

Blue Ribbon Cooking School, www.blueribboncooking.com. This cooking school has instructional intensives, basic classes, and kids classes.

Bon Vivant School of Cooking, www.bon-vivant.com. Located in a private home, classes include a wide range of series classes and single classes on all topics.

Cook's World, www.cooksworld.net. This over-20-year-old cooking store and school offers classes on a wide range of topics.

ART OF THE PIE

Kate McDermott sure has a hold on the pie-making experience. Learn how to perfect your pie-making ability with her interactive class that teaches you all the steps, from what kind of ingredients to use and employing your sense of hearing (yes, hearing), sight, and smell for signs of a perfect pie. Gluten-free pie classes also available. For more information, visit the website: http://artofthepie.com/artofthepie.

Diane's Market Kitchen, www.dianesmarketkitchen.com. Diane's classes are an urban market experience; she'll shop with you through the Pike Place Market and then you'll return to her hidden gem of a cooking school where she'll teach you how to work with the best ingredients around. Small, customized classes give this school an intimate feel.

Dish It Up, http://dish-it-up.com. With two locations in Magnolia and Ballard, this cooking shop and cooking school has a wide range of food-related classes with local chefs.

NuCulinary Asian Cooking School, www.nuculinary.com, offers a series of culinary classes and workshops specializing in Asian techniques and ingredients.

PCC Natural Markets, www.pccnaturalmarkets.com/pcccooks. PCC Cooks provides classes with local food instructors covering a large base of topics, many related to healthy, locavore and organic lifestyles. Kids classes are available as well.

Seattle Free School, www.seattlefreeschool.org, offers a range of free cooking classes on various topics.

The Sizzleworks, www.thesizzleworks.com. This cooking school features intimate hands-on classes with school director Chef Carol, cookbook author and co-host of KCTS 9 Cooks. Sizzleworks offers diverse cuisines taught by expert pastry chefs and local chefs and corporate team events and private parties.

Sur La Table, www.cookingclasses.surlatable .com. This local company, which began in 1972 in the Pike Place Market, has expanded to locations all over the United States. Cooking classes are held at the Kirkland location (90 Central Way, Kirkland, WA 98033; 425-827-554) with famous cookbook authors and both themed and basic classes.

Tom Douglas Culinary Camp, www.tomdouglas .com. Every summer Chef Tom Douglas hosts a culinary camp for adults with gourmet food and the best chefs around. Check the website close to summer for details. (For more about Tom Douglas, see Downtown section, p. 136.)

KID-FRIENDLY SPOTS

Eating out with the little ones in Seattle is actually kind of pleasant (for the parents who have kids at least), many restaurants are kid friendly, and I find that dining in the earlier hours is the best option. With babies and toddlers sometimes it really is about finding places where they can run wild. Here is a round-up of some favorites that actually have kid-designated playing areas.

Vios Cafe & Marketplace, 903 19th Ave. East, Seattle, WA 98112; (206) 329-3236; Capitol Hill; www.vioscafe.com; and **Vios Cafe at Third Place,** 6504 20th Ave. Northeast, Seattle, WA 98115; (206) 525-5701; Ravenna; www.vioscafe.com. See Vios listing, p. 85, for more information.

Twirl Cafe, 2111 Queen Anne Ave. North, Seattle, WA 98109; (206) 283-4552; Queen Anne; www.twirlcafe.com. This modern kids' cafe is where parents chat and kiddos play. Let the kids have fun in the tree house, mini kitchen, or with any of the toys. Supervised kids play is available on certain days so you can steal a few quiet minutes on your computer. They also offer art classes, work-out classes, and a healthy menu that includes natural and organic choices.

Enza Cucina Siciliana, 2128 Queen Anne Ave. North, Seattle, WA 98109; (206) 694-0055; www.enzaseattle.com. This Italian restaurant has a little play kitchen for the cherubs. The food is not always consistent, but the atmosphere is genuine, warm, and comforting like eating at an Italian grandmother's house. All food is housemade from the sauce to the pastas.

Serendipity Cafe, 3222 W. McGraw St., Seattle, WA 98199; (206) 282-YUMM (9866); Magnolia; www.serendipitymagnolia.com. This neighborhood cafe located in Magnolia Village serves American-style comfort food along with a full bar and daily breakfast items. Children can play in the kids' area with trains, toys, and more.

Sugar Rush Baking Company, 4541 California Ave. Southwest, Seattle, WA 98116; (206) 937-1495; West Seattle; www.sugarrushbakingcompany.com. See p. 166 for more information.

Tot Spot Cafe, 17802 134th Ave. Northeast, Suite 6, Woodinville, WA 98072; (425) 488-2795; www.totspotcafe.com. It is a bit of a drive to Woodinville, but what wouldn't you do as parents for a moment of sanity and a few minutes of kids running wild with toys everywhere? They have a 600-square-foot play area, with supervised play and a drop-off care option.

Madrona Eatery & Ale House, 1138 34th Ave., Seattle, WA 98122; (206) 323-7807; Madrona; **Montlake Ale House,** 2307 24th Ave. East, Seattle, WA 98112; (206) 726-5968; Montlake; and **Pied Piper Ale House,** 2404 N.E. 65th St., Seattle, WA 98115; (206) 729-0603; Ravenna. Let it be known that a beer with some friends is the perfect solution to temper tantrums, growing pains, and other parental "dilemmas." These three establishments—same owner—don't feel kiddie-like at all; no bright colors or balloons here, but both the Madrona Alehouse and Montlake Alehouse have lots of toys and a designated kids area. Pied Pier may not have the same size playing area, but it has lots of toys and books and it is definitely kid-friendly.

Firehouse Coffee, 2622 N.W. Market St., Seattle, WA 98107; (206) 784-2911; Ballard. Located right next door to the **Gymboree** kids classes (Gymboree Play & Music, 2622 N.W. Market St., Seattle, WA 98107; 206-783-3741; Ballard; www.gymboreeclasses.com), this is how you kill two birds with one stone. Bring your baby, waddler, or toddler to a class next door, let them run after Gymbo the clown, and then head to Firehouse with a friend for some coffee while the kids explore the toys in the kids area. Way to guarantee a nap for your kid and for yourself.

The University of Washington Experimental College, www
.depts.washington.edu/asuwxpcl, offers brief 1- to 3-week classes
on niche cooking subjects. They cost from $20 to $100. New courses
are offered every 3 months.

Whole Foods Market, www.wholefoodsmarket.com. Whole Foods
Market has cooking classes on a range of topics, including special
allergy and dietary lifestyle–related classes.

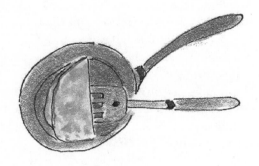

Recipes

Get ready for your own dinner party. In true Seattle-style, we like to host and get people around the table. One of the simple pleasures in this city is using the abundance of ingredients—the seasonal surprises that you can find at farmers' markets—to host your own dinner. In this chapter, local chefs and bakers give you a backstage pass to their favorite recipes. You'll find easy appetizers, main courses, and sweet desserts.

Citrus 75

Local celebrity chef, mixologist, and author Kathy Casey owns two Dish D'lish cafes (see p. xxiii) located in Seattle-Tacoma International Airport (aka Sea-Tac Airport), where you can grab healthy breakfasts and lunches as well as snacks and creative food gifts. She also has a private food studio in Ballard where she hosts events. Chef Kathy is considered a pioneer in the chef-bar movement, concocting cocktails for TV appearances, restaurants, hotels, and her nine cookbooks. Here Chef Kathy's mixology expertise comes into play as she shares her recipe for Citrus 75 featuring Liquid Kitchen™ 5130 Honey—available, with other products, at www .kathycasey.com. For tasty variations on this recipe add fresh rosemary muddled with the clementine, or substitute a few fresh berries for the clementine in the summer.

Makes 1 drink

½ or ¼ clementine or mandarin, depending upon size

1½ ounce local gin

½ ounce House-made Limoncello (recipe follows)

¾ ounce fresh lemon juice

½ ounce Liquid Kitchen™ Honey Syrup (recipe follows)

1 ounce brut Champagne

Garnish: Lemon zest twist or thin slice of clementine

Place the clementine into a mixing glass. Muddle to release the juices. Measure in the gin, limoncello, lemon juice, and honey syrup. Fill with ice. Cap and shake vigorously.

Strain into a martini glass. Add a splash of Champagne. Garnish with a lemon zest twist or a thin slice of clementine.

Liquid Kitchen™ Honey Syrup

Measure 1 part hot water and 1 part Liquid Kitchen™ 5130 Honey into a container. Stir until honey is completely dissolved. Store refrigerated for up to 2 weeks.

House-made Limoncello

Makes about 2½ cups

3 lemons
1½ cups citrus vodka

¾ cups sugar
½ cup water

With a potato peeler, peel the zest from the lemons, being sure not to get any white pith. Place the lemon peel in a clean 4-cup glass jar with lid. (Use the rest of the lemon for another purpose.) Add the citrus vodka.

Cap the jars and shake well. Let sit at room temperature for 1 week, shaking the jars every couple of days.

After 1 week, bring the sugar and water to a boil in a large saucepan, stirring to dissolve the sugar. Boil for 2 minutes, then let cool to room temperature.

Strain the vodka into a big bowl. Stir the cooled sugar syrup into the strained liquor. At this point, you can bottle your limoncello into fancy bottles or clean, clear wine bottles. Cap tightly and store at room temperature for up to 2 months, or refrigerated for 1 year.

Recipe courtesy of Chef Kathy Casey.

Jackie's Tomatoes with Avocado-Skordalia

Chef Tom Douglas calls his wife and business partner, Jackie Cross, the "Farmer-in-Chief" of their farm in Prosser, Washington where they grow produce for the Tom Douglas Restaurants (see Etta's on p. 141, Lola on p. 129, Dahlia Bakery on p. 98, Dahlia Lounge on p. 140, Dahlia Workshop on p. 3, Palace Kitchen p.145, and Serious Pie on p. 132; also see sidebar about Tom Douglas on p. 136). He created this appetizer for Seatown SeaBar & Rotisserie (p. 131) to show off Prosser's luscious, peak of season, ripe tomatoes. Skordalia in Greek cuisine is a thick sauce or dip made with minced garlic and a bulky base. In this case, bread is used as a thickener. This appetizer dish is great alongside fried fish or vegetables or just on its own as a way to savor the simplicity of the tomatoes.

Note: It's important to use a loaf of European-style rustic bread for this recipe.

Serves 6 to 8 as an appetizer

- ½ loaf rustic bread, crusts removed, cut into large chunks (about 12 ounces of bread before crusts are removed)
- 1 teaspoon red wine vinegar
- ¼ cup freshly squeezed lemon juice, plus more to taste
- 1 egg yolk
- 1½ teaspoons minced garlic
- ¼ cup extra-virgin olive oil
- Kosher salt or sea salt to taste
- 1 ripe avocado, peeled and pitted
- 3 ripe, flavorful tomatoes, cored and sliced horizontally

To make the skordalia, put the bread in a bowl and cover with cold water. Let sit 10 minutes, weighted with a plate to keep the bread submerged. Drain the bread in a sieve, then use your hands to squeeze out as much of the water as possible. Put the bread, vinegar, lemon juice, egg yolk, and garlic in the bowl of a food processor. Process until well combined. With the motor running, gradually add the oil through the feed tube until the mixture is smooth. Season to taste with salt.

In a large bowl, mash the avocado, using a potato masher or a wooden spoon. Add the skordalia and mix with a rubber spatula until well combined. Taste and season with more salt and lemon juice if needed.

Spread the avocado-skordalia on a platter and arrange the tomato slices on top. Sprinkle the tomatoes with salt to taste and then serve.

Recipe courtesy of Chef Tom Douglas.

Caramelized Apples with Seattle Six Spice & Alder Smoked Salt

These caramelized apples from World Spice Merchants (p. 123) are a versatile dish, equally at home alongside roasted pork or vanilla ice cream. They are only slightly sweet, with intricate spicing that tickles the palate with far-reaching flavors. The Alder Smoked Salt is available for purchase at the store. It adds a smoky and salty flavor to food without added heat.

6 tablespoons butter

3 large apples (Honeycrisp, Fuji, or Gala), cored and sliced into ½-inch wedges (about 6 cups)

4 tablespoons brown sugar, divided in half

2 teaspoons ground Seattle Six Spice (recipe below)

⅔ cup apple cider

½ teaspoon Alder Smoked Salt

Makes 3 to 4 servings

Melt the butter in a large skillet over medium heat. Add the apples to the pan and sprinkle with 2 tablespoons brown sugar. Sauté the apples, stirring frequently, for 6 to 8 minutes, until they just start to become tender.

Combine the remaining 2 tablespoons brown sugar with Seattle Six Spice and sprinkle over the apples. Toss the mixture gently and cook over medium heat for an additional 3 to 5 minutes, until the sugar begins to caramelize and the apples are crisp-tender.

Remove the apples from the skillet to a serving dish using a slotted spoon. Increase heat and pour the apple cider into the skillet, scraping up any browned bits. Reduce the heat slightly and simmer for 1 to 3 minutes, until the sauce has reduced and thickened slightly. Pour the finished sauce over the warm apples and garnish evenly with Alder Smoked Salt. Serve immediately.

Seattle Six Spice

Keep a little of this spice blend around to use as a base for meat rubs in addition to the caramelized apples above and anything else that might come to mind. Inspired by the classic five-spice blends in Asian cuisine, it has a home in any kitchen. It is recommended to buy these spices whole and grind them after they are toasted. To grind the spices, use a coffee grinder or a mortar and pestle.

3 teaspoons Tellicherry black pepper
4 teaspoons cumin seed
4 teaspoons coriander seed

3 teaspoons fennel seed
4 teaspoons star anise, whole
7 teaspoons orange peel, dried

Toast pepper, cumin, coriander, and fennel in a dry pan over medium high heat until lightly browned and fragrant for about 2 to 4 minutes. Allow to cool and mix in star anise and orange peel. Store in whole form for freshness and grind just before use.

Recipe courtesy of World Spice Merchants.

Apricot Mostarda di Cremona

Chef Jason Stratton of Spinasse (p. 81) creates food focused on the techniques of the Piedmont region of Italy combined with the artisan producers and natural ingredients that are characteristic of the Northwest. Here he shares a recipe for Mostarda Di Cremona, a condiment traditionally made of whole fruits candied in spicy mustard syrup. In this rendition he makes it with apricot. This condiment is traditionally served as an accompaniment for braised or roasted meats but it is also delicious alongside your favorite cheese.

Makes about 10 to 14 portions

2 pounds apricots, washed
4 cups cold water
4 cups sugar
¼ cup dry mustard
1 tablespoon ground cayenne pepper

1 cup Champagne vinegar
3 tablespoons brown mustard seed
Salt to taste

Gently pack the apricots into a clean wide-mouth glass jar or a few jars, leaving 1½ inches of headspace. Stir water and sugar together in a pot and bring to a boil to make a simple syrup.

Meanwhile, put the dry mustard and cayenne in a bowl. Whisk the vinegar into the dry mustard mixture to make a slurry.

Heat a pan over medium heat and toast the mustard seed until it begins to smell aromatic. The seeds will start to gray and pop. Add immediately to the simple syrup.

Slowly stir the vinegar mustard slurry into the simple syrup. Season well with salt and re-taste the mixture. It should be quite tart, sweet, and well-seasoned with salt.

Pour the hot syrup directly over the fruit to cover completely. Press a piece of parchment into the top of the jar and weight with a small ramekin or a couple of small saucers. Refrigerate.

This mostarda improves greatly upon sitting for a week and lasts for quite awhile, provided that the fruit is submerged.

Recipe courtesy of Chef Jason Stratton.

Gnocchetti with Pancetta, Spring Onions & English Peas

Chef Ethan Stowell is the owner, along with his wife Angela Stowell, of Staple
& Fancy Mercantile (p. 33), Anchovies & Olives (p. 63), Tavolata (p. 135),
and How to Cook a Wolf (p. 71) as well as creator of a homemade line of pasta
products called Lagana Foods. Here Chef.Stowell shares his recipe for a warm
pasta dish with gnocchetti, a smaller version of gnocchi.

Serves 4

- ½ pound dried *gnocchetti sardi*
- 2 tablespoons extra-virgin olive oil, plus more for drizzling
- ½ pound pancetta, cut into small dice
- ½ pound spring onions, cleaned and sliced
- 3 medium cloves garlic, peeled and thinly sliced
- ½ cup English peas, blanched until tender

- Pinch of dried red chile flakes
- Kosher salt and freshly ground pepper
- 2 tablespoons fresh mint, chopped
- 2 tablespoons fresh parsley, chopped
- Parmigiano-Reggiano, for serving

Bring a large pot of lightly salted water to a rolling boil. Add the pasta and cook
for about 12 minutes, or 1 minute less than the package directions.

While the pasta is cooking, heat 2 tablespoons olive oil in a sauté pan over medium heat. Add the diced pancetta and sauté until some of the fat renders and the pancetta is golden. You don't want it to become too crisp. Add the spring onions and sauté for 5 to 6 minutes, stirring occasionally to prevent sticking. When the spring onions are golden, add the sliced garlic and English peas and cook 1 minute longer. Add the dried chile flakes. When the pasta is done, drain and add to the onion, English peas, and pancetta mixture, adding a couple of tablespoons of reserved gnochetti cooking water if the mixture seems dry. Season to taste with salt and pepper. Add the mint and parsley and toss. Place in a serving bowl. Drizzle olive oil over the top. Using a vegetable peeler, shave a few large curls of Parmigiano-Reggiano on top. Serve and enjoy!

Recipe courtesy of Chef Ethan Stowell.

Apple Wood Grilled Spot Prawns

Here Chef Mark Fuller of Spring Hill (p. 174) shares his recipe for this sauté of shrimp, morels, creamy grits, a poached egg, and shrimp gravy. Spot prawns are large shrimp frequently harvested from the Pacific Ocean along the West Coast of the United States and Canada. They have a firm texture and a sweet delicate flavor. Call ahead to see if they are available at your favorite seafood store. The recipe is a bit challenging, but well worth the effort!

Serves 8

Creamy Grits

850 grams / 30 ounces water

176 grams / 6.2 ounces Anson Mills course white grits (available online or you can substitute another high quality brand such as Bob's Red Mill)

100 grams / 3.5 ounces crème fraîche

250 grams / 9 ounces Beecher's White Cheddar (see p. 100)

100 grams / 3.5 ounces Parmesan cheese

Kosher salt

Black pepper

To make the grits, bring the water to a boil and slowly stir in the grits with a wooden spoon. Continue to stir until the water returns to a boil. Reduce the heat to low and simmer and stir occasionally for 2½ hours.

Once the grits are cooked, add the crème fraîche, cheddar, and Parmesan. Season with kosher salt and black pepper. Keep warm.

Mise en place

Poaching water for eggs

8 chicken eggs

3 pounds spot prawns, peeled and skewered, shells reserved (this should be enough for 8 skewers, 3 to 5 shrimp per skewer)

One Recipe Creamy Grits*

160 grams / 5.64 ounces morel mushrooms, brushed clean and sliced

60 grams / 2 ounces unsalted butter

Small lemon, cut in half

One Recipe Shrimp Gravy*

Scallion, sliced very thin

Sea salt

Shrimp Gravy

Reserved shrimp shells

170 grams / 6 ounces heavy whipping cream

85 grams / 3 ounces unsalted butter

10 grams / 0.35 ounces Worcestershire sauce

Kosher salt

Black pepper

Make shrimp stock with the shells. Reduce the stock to au sec or until almost completely evaporated. Add the heavy cream and reduce by one-third on medium heat. Whisk in the butter and season with the Worcestershire, salt, and pepper.

Strain and hold warm.

To Assemble

Bring a pot of water to a simmer for poaching the eggs. Heat a grill to hot or medium hot. Once you have all of your mise en place, *your poaching water is simmering, and your grill is hot, crack your eggs into individual ramekins.*

Over medium-high heat, sauté the morel mushrooms with the butter, finish with a small squeeze of lemon, salt, and pepper. Reserve and keep warm.

Gently pour the eggs out of the ramekins into the poaching liquid and poach the eggs.

Place the shrimp on the grill over medium-high heat. Depending on the size of the shrimp, they will most likely finish cooking before the egg is done. Allow the shrimp to rest off the heat while the eggs finish cooking.

When the eggs are done, place them on a paper towel and remove the loose albumen.

Plating

Place a spoonful of hot grits on eight individual plates.

Spoon some of the sautéed morel mushrooms alongside the grits.

Rest one poached egg on each spoonful of grits.

Remove the shrimp from the skewers and place tightly around the egg.

Garnish the egg with the sliced scallion and sea salt.

Drizzle with a generous amount of shrimp gravy.

Recipe courtesy of Chef Mark Fuller.

Vegetarian Strata

This dish from the Essential Baking Company (p. 5), made with their delicious potato bread, is a great option for vegetarians to enjoy. The combination of textures and flavors makes a hearty and heartwarming meal.

Serves 4

- 1 loaf of potato bread
- ⅔ cup sliced leeks
- ⅔ cup chopped onion
- 4 or 5 mushrooms, cleaned and chopped
- 1 cup fresh or frozen peas
- Salt and pepper to taste
- 4 large eggs
- ¼ cup milk
- ½ cup shredded Gruyère, optional
- Butter

Preheat oven to 350 degrees and grease an 8-inch square baking dish. Cut the potato loaf into ½-inch pieces and combine with the leeks, onions, mushrooms, and peas. Add salt and pepper to taste.

Fill the baking dish with the bread and vegetables. Whisk the eggs and milk together and pour over the ingredients in the dish. (You can substitute vegetable broth for the egg and milk for a vegan dish; use just enough to moisten the bread.) Press down on the mixture with a spatula, making sure that all of the liquid soaks into the bread. Sprinkle Gruyère or your favorite cheese on top, if desired.

Cover and bake for 30 minutes or until the strata is cooked through, when a knife inserted in the center comes clean. Remove the cover and bake an additional 10–15 minutes until golden brown. Remove from the oven and let set for 5 minutes. Serve warm. **Tip:** This can be prepared a day early and refrigerated overnight.

Recipe courtesy of the Essential Baking Company.

Sashimi Salmon with Argan Oil

Mustapha Haddouch's Moroccan Argan Oil (see Mustapha's Fine Foods, p. 60) complements the flavor of sashimi-grade wild King Salmon. This is a simple recipe that can be assembled in just a few minutes.

Here is part of Mustapha's explanation about the oil from his website: "Argan oil is a deep golden oil, often with a reddish tinge that is produced from the seeds of the Argan tree, which only grows in Morocco."

It is a light weight oil with a nutty, toasty, spicy feel, a unique and memorable flavor essential to the Berber cuisine of Southwest Morocco.

Serves 8 to 10

2 pounds sashimi-grade wild king salmon
Fleur de sel to taste

2 tablespoons lemon juice
5 tablespoons argan oil

Slice salmon thinly and plate.

Sprinkle the fleur de sel on the salmon.

Make a dressing of 1 part lemon juice and 3 parts argan oil.

Drizzle the dressing on the salmon just before serving.

Recipe courtesy of Mustapha's Fine Foods of Morocco.

Halibut Ceviche with Mango and Cucumber

This recipe is from Chef Thierry Rautureau, the Chef in the Hat, owner of Rover's (p. 90) and Luc (p. 74). Serve this appetizer in a martini glass at your next party. Wine pairing: Viognier.

Serves 4 to 6

1 pound halibut

Halibut Marinade

½ cup freshly squeezed lime juice

¼ cup seasoned rice vinegar

1 medium red onion, sliced thin

4 garlic cloves, peeled and crushed

1 ounce olive oil

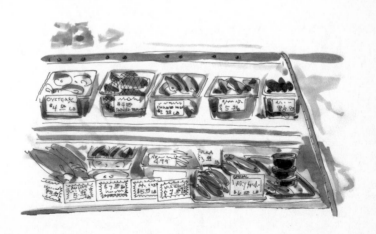

Garnish

1 mango, peeled and cut into small dice

1 English cucumber, peeled and cut into small dice

1 small jalapeño, minced fine (to taste depending on how hot you want it)

1 teaspoon each of fresh cilantro and lemon balm, chopped (¼ of a teaspoon of grated lemon zest could be used as a substitute)

Sea salt and white pepper to taste

Cut the halibut into ¼ to ½-inch cubes. Place the cubes in a glass or stainless steel container.

Mix the marinade ingredients, pour over the halibut, and toss to coat. Cover and refrigerate for at least 1 hour and not more than 2 hours.

About 30 minutes before serving, add the mango, cucumber, jalapeño, cilantro, and lemon balm. Mix all together. Adjust the seasoning with sea salt and white pepper. Chill well. Serve next to garden greens or in a martini glass.

Recipe courtesy of Chef Thierry Rautureau.

Golden Beet Risotto

Kurt Beecher Dammeier is the mastermind behind Beecher's Handmade Cheese (p. 100), Maximus/Minimus (p. xxv), Bennett's Pure Food Bistro (p. 222), and Pasta & Co (p. 16). Here he shares the recipe for a Golden Beet Risotto that is served at Bennett's Pure Food Bistro and made with Beecher's cheese.

Serves 4 as a main course or 6 as an appetizer

- **4 cups low-sodium store-bought chicken broth**
- **2 tablespoons unsalted butter**
- **2 tablespoons extra-virgin olive oil**
- **1 small sweet onion, peeled and minced**
- **½ teaspoon kosher salt, or more to taste**
- **¾ pound golden beets, peeled and coarsely shredded**
- **1½ cups Arborio rice**
- **2 ounces Beecher's Flagship cheese, grated (about 1¼ cups)**
- **¼ teaspoon turmeric**
- **Salt to taste**

In a medium saucepan, heat the chicken stock to a simmer over medium heat. Reduce the heat to the lowest heat possible to keep the stock warm until you are ready to use it.

In a large heavy-bottomed skillet (at least 10 inches wide), heat the butter and olive oil over medium heat until the butter melts. Add the onion and salt. Sauté until the onion softens, about 3 minutes. Add the beets and sauté, stirring frequently, for 10 minutes or until the pan is dry. Transfer half of the beet mixture to a small bowl and set aside.

Add the rice to the skillet and cook for 3 minutes, stirring frequently to coat the rice with oil. Ladle 1 cup of the hot stock over the rice and stir frequently. When *all of the liquid has been absorbed and your stirring spoon leaves a trail showing where it ran across the bottom of the pot, ladle in another 1 cup of liquid, stirring until the liquid has been absorbed. Continue adding stock until the rice grains are al dente and pleasantly creamy, about 30 minutes total. You might not use all the stock; it will depend on the rice.*

Stir in the cheese, reserved beet mixture, and turmeric. Taste for seasoning and add salt as needed. Serve immediately.

Recipe courtesy of Kurt Beecher Dammeier.

Green Tea Checkerboard Cookies

Etsuko Minematsu and Keiji Koh, owners of Fresh Flours (p. 6), have generously shared their recipe for these delightful and pretty tea cookies. Characteristic of Japanese pastries, they are much less sweet than many American pastries. A perfect accompaniment to a cup of tea. The matcha powder can be purchased at Uwajimaya Market (p. 122).

Makes about 40 cookies

Vanilla Dough

⅔ cup unsalted butter, softened
1¼ cup powdered sugar
1 egg
1 teaspoon vanilla extract

2 cups sifted all-purpose flour
¼ teaspoon salt, mixed with flour

Green Tea Dough

⅔ cup unsalted butter, softened
1¼ cup cup powdered sugar
1 egg
1 teaspoon vanilla extract
1¾ cups sifted all-purpose flour

¼ teaspoon salt, mixed with flour
¼ cup sifted matcha (green tea) powder, mixed with flour

To make the Vanilla Dough, cream the butter and powdered sugar until light and fluffy. Add egg and vanilla extract, and beat until well blended. Add flour-salt mixture and mix until fully incorporated. Wrap in plastic wrap and chill in the fridge more than 1 hour.

To make the Green Tea Dough, repeat above directions using the Green Tea Dough ingredients.

On a lightly floured surface, using a pizza wheel or knife and a ruler, cut out five 8½ x ½ x ½-inch strips from the green dough, and four strips in same size from the vanilla dough.

Place three strips of dough on plastic covered surface, alternating vanilla and green strips (green-vanilla-green).

Brush tops and in between the strips with water. Gently press strips together. Repeat, forming second and third layers, alternating colors to create a checkerboard effect. Wrap assembled log in plastic. Freeze for 15 minutes.

Preheat oven to 350 degrees. Slice each log into ⅜-inch-thick slices; place on baking sheet. Bake for around 15 minutes or until brown around the edges.

Recipe courtesy of Etsuko Minematsu and Keiji Koh.

Maria Hines's Chocolate Ganache Cakes

Maria Hines, owner of Tilth (p. 35) and Golden Beetle (p. 25) shares her recipe here for these decadent individual chocolate cakes. These are a great way to impress your guests. Serve them with Domaine Pietri-Geraud Banyuls (dried strawberry, toasted nuts, caramel), chocolate sauce, chantilly, and fleur de sel.

4 tasting servings

For the cake

28 grams / 1 ounce unsalted butter

26.8 grams / 2 tablespoons sugar

13.2 grams / ½ ounce water

20.8 grams / ⅛ cup bittersweet chocolate

20.8 grams / ⅛ cup milk chocolate

2 grams (pinch) sugar

18 grams (1 ea.) whole eggs

10 grams (1 ea.) egg yolks

9.2 grams / 1 tablespoon all-purpose flour

Pinch of salt

Muffin tray (Use 4 servings of tray or 4 ramekins)

For the ganache

42 grams / ¼ cup heavy cream

56 grams / 2 ounces milk chocolate, finely chopped

For the chantilly

100 grams / 6½ tablespoons heavy cream

16 grams / 2 tablespoons powdered sugar, sifted

20.8 grams / ⅛ cup bittersweet chocolate, finely chopped

For the Cake Batter

Heat butter, 2 tablespoons sugar, and water in saucepan. Bring to a boil then simmer until butter is melted and sugar is dissolved.

Pour over chocolate and stir until chocolate is melted and well blended.

Whisk eggs and egg yolks in remaining sugar in stand mixer until mixture forms a thick ribbon-like strand. Add chocolate mixture to eggs and stir until well blended.

Add flour and salt, blend well, and refrigerate at least 1 hour or overnight.

For the Ganache

Heat heavy cream in a double boiler and slowly whisk in chopped chocolate until completely melted. Chill until cold.

To Bake the Cake

Roll ganache into ½-ounce balls and chill until cold.

Fill muffin tin molds or ramekins one-third full with batter and place a ganache ball in the center of each.

Cover each with additional cake batter and smooth the tops. Each mold should be three-fourths full.

Bake at 350 degrees until sides are set, tops puffed but still soft, about 15 minutes.

Remove from the oven, let cool 2 minutes, and invert onto sheet pan.

For the Chantilly

Whisk cream until soft peaks form, then whisk in powdered sugar and chocolate. Garnish the cake with fleur du sel and top with the Chantilly.

Recipe courtesy of Maria Hines.

Brown Butter Bars

This recipe is courtesy of Pastry Chef Heather Earnhardt of Volunteer Park Cafe (p. 85).

Browning the butter really increases the flavor and adds a nuttiness to it. Ooh and the aroma in the kitchen! These are a perfect treat along with a glass of milk or wrapped up as a gift for friends.

Yield: 16 bars

- **12 ounces unsalted butter**
- **2¼ cups unbleached all-purpose flour**
- **1½ teaspoons baking powder**
- **1½ teaspoons kosher salt**
- **3 extra-large eggs**
- **2 cups packed light-brown sugar**
- **1 tablespoon vanilla extract**
- **1 cup pecan pieces**
- **1 cup toffee bits**

Preheat oven to 325 degrees. Butter a 10 x 10-inch baking pan. Line bottom of pan with parchment paper. Butter and flour the parchment paper.

In a saucepan over medium heat, melt the butter and continue to simmer until it turns a deep golden brown; remove from heat and let cool to room temperature. Sift together flour, baking powder, and salt. Set aside.

In the bowl of an electric mixer, using the paddle attachment, combine eggs and sugar. Beat on medium-high speed until light and fluffy, about 3 minutes. Add vanilla and beat to combine. Drizzle in melted browned butter. Scrape bowl. Add flour mixture, then pecan pieces and toffee bits. Mix until combined. Pour into prepared pan.

Bake until a cake tester inserted in the center comes out clean, 35 to 40 minutes (do not overbake), rotating halfway through baking time. Cool to room temperature before cutting.

Recipe courtesy of Pastry Chef Heather Earnhardt.

Sugar Rush Baking Company Scones

Every household needs a recipe for scones, and Sugar Rush Baking Company (p. 166) agreed to share their basic scone recipe. These taste great with butter and jam. Other variations: Add cheddar, blueberries, chocolate chips, or peaches to the batter.

Makes 6 scones

2 cups flour
⅓ cup granulated sugar
1 teaspoon baking powder
¼ teaspoon baking soda
½ teaspoon salt

½ cup cold unsalted butter, cubed
1 egg
½ cup buttermilk

Preheat oven to 325 degrees.

Combine the first 5 ingredients in a medium-size mixing bowl.

Using a pastry blender, cut in cold butter until mixture resembles coarse crumbs.

If possible, use a digital scale to weigh the egg and buttermilk out to 6 ounces, mix together and pour into the dry mixture. If you don't have access to a scale, you can use the above measurements, and add buttermilk as needed.

Using a wooden spoon, mix until all ingredients come together and form a wet shaggy dough ball.

Turn dough out onto a lightly floured surface and knead, 5 or 6 times.

Form the dough into a ball and flatten it into an 8-inch disk, slightly raised in the center.

Cut the disk in half, and each half into thirds, resembling pie slices.

Place scones on a lined cookie sheet and bake 9 minutes at 325 degrees.

Turn scones 180 degrees and continue to bake for 5 minutes.

Check scones: A wooden skewer should come out clean, or they should be firm to the touch, and slightly browned along the edges, not golden! If more time is needed, put them in for 5 more minutes, but watch carefully.

Recipe courtesy of Sugar Rush Baking Company.

Microwaved Chocolate Sponge Cake

This creative recipe demonstrates the fun that Chef Brian McCracken and Chef Dana Tough have in the kitchen at Spur Gastropub (p. 132) and Tavern Law (p. 82)! You will need a whipped cream siphon that can be found at any specialty kitchen store such as Sur La Table. You will also need paper cups.

Yield: 8 servings

1 ounce milk chocolate

2 ounces dark chocolate

3 egg whites

1 egg yolk

½ cup granulated sugar

½ cup canola oil

Pinch of salt

½ cup pastry (or cake) flour, sifted

Paper cups

Optional: vanilla or caramel ice cream and caramel sauce for serving

Place chocolate in microwave-safe bowl. Melt chocolate in microwave for 1½ minutes, or until fully melted.

Meanwhile, place eggs, sugar, oil, and salt into a blender, and blend for 30 seconds. Add melted chocolate and blend for another 30 seconds.

Pour into mixing bowl and then whisk sifted flour into mixture.

Immediately pour into 1-pint-size whipped cream siphon. Screw on lid, add 1 nitrous oxide (N_2O) cartridge. Shake and let sit for 30 minutes at room temperature.

Fill an 8-ounce paper cup half full with batter, and microwave on high for 40 seconds until the cake is slightly firm to touch and has little holes in it.

Let sit for 1 minute, and serve immediately with vanilla or caramel ice cream and your favorite caramel sauce.

Recipe courtesy of Chef Brian McCracken and Chef Dana Tough.

Food Fests
& Events

Seattle is a very food-oriented city and there are many food-centric events and festivals going on, especially in the summer. There are too many events to mention them all here, so below are a few for you to nibble on. All events are listed in the month they usually occur.

January/February

Chinatown/International District's Lunar New Year Celebration, www.cidbia.org/events. A fun celebration for all! Dates vary year to year.

Events that are national events but locally-loved

February

*Cochon 555, www.cochon555.com/menu/2011-tour-dates/ 220-seattle. The event dedicated to all things swine is a marriage of 5 Chefs, 5 Pigs, and 5 Winemakers.

Seattle Food and Wine Experience, http://seattlefoodandwine experience.com. This one day event features lots of wine, beer, and food.

March

Taste Washington, http://tastewashington.org. The Washington State Wine Commission's event is a weekend of wine- and food-related seminars, restaurant food, and chef demos. The event kicks off with the Washington Wine Restaurant Awards (www.washington wine.org/restaurantawards).

Foodportunity is a series of networking and educational events connecting food writers, restaurateurs, farmers, food companies, and all food-passionate people. The top restaurants and companies in town serve bites, and lasting connections are made while networking over food. Get on the mailing list for more information at www.foodportunity.com.

Vegfest, www.vegofwa.org/vegfest. The Vegetarians of Washington present this vegetarian festival with food samples, demos, and everything coming up in the vegetarian world.

April

Food as Art, www.cdforum.org/food-as-art. Food as Art is the coming together of Seattle's top African American Chefs and restaurateurs to raise funds for the Central District Forum for Arts & Ideas—Seattle's Black Arts and Culture Presenter.

Voracious Tasting, www.seattleweekly.com/voracioustasting. *Seattle Weekly*'s Voracious Tasting & Food Awards is an evening filled with restaurant bites, a chef showdown, and the *Seattle Weekly*'s food awards.

May

Seattle Cheese Festival, www.seattlecheesefestival.com. Every May, for two full days, Pike Place Market turns into a cheese oasis with loads of free cheese samples, cooking demonstrations, and a fresh mozzarella making demo.

*****Seattle Luxury Chocolate Salon,** www.seattlechocolatesalon .com. If you believe that you can never have too much chocolate then this event can't be missed.

June

Washington Brewers Festival, www.washingtonbeer.com/event wabf.htm. A three-day event showcasing all the beers you can possibly think of plus cider and wine tastings as well as live entertainment.

July

Bite of Seattle, www.comcastbiteofseattle.com. Every summer this three-day food festival brings together lots of restaurants, live entertainment, and food companies. Don't miss "The Alley," hosted by Tom Douglas and benefiting Food Lifeline, where $10 will get you a taste from Seattle favorites. Come early because lines are long.

Burning Beast, www.burningbeast.com. Local chefs team up to prepare an animal, vegetable, or sea creature out in the wilderness for the ultimate bonfire and outdoor event.

Chinatown-International District Summer Festival, www .cidbia.org/events. It's cultural dances, live music, a karaoke contest and booths featuring Asian food and crafts at this annual two-day event.

Farestart's Guest Chef on the Waterfront, www.farestart.org/ help/events/waterfront/index.html. It is an evening of food, wine, and beer all to benefit the job training and placement program at Farestart.

CELEBRATING BASTILLE DAY!

Bastille Day is celebrated in this town and kicks off with an event at Seattle Center including live concerts, French culture, bistro food, and a wine garden. For info go to www.seattle-bastille.org/index.htm.

Cafe Campagne (p. 125) located in the Pike Place Market holds its own outdoor street festival on July 14, rain or shine with live music, French street food, and lots of wine. Down the street, **Le Pichet** (p. 128) has live music, celebrations, and French fare. The romantic **Maximilien** (81A Pike Street, Seattle, WA 98101; 206-682-7270; www.maximilienrestaurant.com; Pike Place Market) usually celebrates with live music and a Bastille Day dinner menu.

August

Auction of Washington Wines, www.auctionofwashingtonwines .org. This charity wine auction includes a picnic with winemakers, wine dinners at private estates and wineries, and a Grand Gala Auction under the big tent on the Chateau Ste Michelle Winery grounds, where some of Seattle's chefs prepare a six-course culinary extravaganza.

Chinatown/International District Night Market, www.cidbia .org/events. It is a night party, where you get to shop, dine, and peruse through this culturally rich district while enjoying live entertainment and movies.

Ferragosto at La Spiga, www
.laspiga.com. Every year, Capitol
Hill's La Spiga (p. 74) celebrates
Ferragosto, an Italian holiday with
unlimited food, wine, and music.

**Incredible   Feast—Where
the Farmers are the Stars,**
www.seattlefarmersmarkets.org/
the-incredible-feast-where-the-farmers-are
-the-stars. The neighborhood Farmers market
alliance is where local chefs and local farms team
up to support the Good Farmer Fund and the Neighborhood Farmers
Market Alliance (see chapter on farmers market for more about
them).

Sunset Supper, http://pikeplacemarketfoundation.org/events
/sunsetsupper.shtml. It's dining and dancing at this Pike Place
Market festival with lots of restaurants, breweries, and wineries to
choose from.

October

Fremont's Oktoberfest, www.fremontoktoberfest.com. This is a
celebration of all the brew you can drink, activities, and more.

*Lamb Jam, http://fansoflambseattle.com/lambjamseattle.aspx. For the love of lamb, this yearly event brings together local chefs and has them cook up lamb in many creative ways.

Pike Place Market Artisan Food Festival, www.pikeplace market.org/news_events/events_promotions. Browse through the market tasting food, watching chef demos, enjoying a beer, exploring a wine garden, and listening to live music.

November

Elliot's Oyster Bash, www.elliottsoysterhouse.com. Every year Elliot's (p. 140) hosts a big oyster bash with over 30 varieties of oysters, a seafood buffet, and live entertainment.

Taste of Tulalip, www.tulalipresort.com/entertainment/taste-of -tulalip.aspx. This two-day event at Tulalip Resort Casino features the finest Washington wines paired with food from this luxurious resort's team of chefs.

December

Winter Beer Fest, www.washingtonbeer.com/festival_winter .htm. One of the many events put on by the Washington Beer Commission, showcasing beers and breweries around the state.

Take a Walk on the Eastside

If you hear Seattleites talking about the Eastside, they are refer-
ring to the suburbs just east of Seattle. As a home for the offices of
many large companies, including our own Microsoft, it has become
a place for the employees to settle with their families. In the last
few years, new restaurants have opened up in these areas, and a
whole new dining scene is beginning to emerge.

On Mercer Island, **Bennett's Pure Food Bistro** (7650 S.E. 27th
St., Mercer Island, WA 98040; 206-232-2759; www.bennettsbistro
.com; $$$) is a neighborhood bistro serving brunch, lunch, and
dinner with wholesome and pure ingredients that are fresh and sea-
sonal. See Kurt Beecher Dammeier's recipe for **Golden Beet Risotto**
(served at Bennett's Pure Food Bistro and made with Beecher's
cheese) on p. 205. Some of Seattle's popular restaurants have set up
shops on the Eastside, too. You can find **Cantinetta** (see p. 22) with
handmade Italian pasta dishes and seasonal ingredients and modern

Vietnamese food at **Monsoon East** (see p. 87), with the Eastside location boasting an almost full-day happy hour Sunday through Thursday, 3 to 10 p.m. The upscale mall known as the Bravern houses favorites like **John Howie Steak** (11111 N.E. 8th St., Suite 125, Bellevue, WA 98004; 425-440-0880; www.johnhowiesteak.com; $$$$), which serves custom-aged USDA prime steak, American Kobe, and Japanese Waygu beef with nightly live piano performances in the lounge, and **Wild Ginger** (11020 N.E. 6th St., Suite 90, Bellevue, WA 98004; 425-495-8889; www.wildginger.net; $$; see website for additional location), a landmark restaurant where Southeast Asia and the Northwest merge with dim sum and family-style dining.

Seafood enthusiasts will love the raw bar and selection of seafood at **Sea Star Restaurant & Raw Bar** (205 108th Ave. Northeast, Bellevue, WA 98004; 425-456-0010; www.seastarrestaurant.com; $$; see website for additional location), also owned by Chef John Howie. **Boom Noodle** (504 Bellevue Sq., Bellevue, WA 98004; 425-453-6094; www.boomnoodle.com; $; see website for additional locations) serves Japanese fare with small plates and hearty bowls of noodles like ramen and soba.

For a "gastropub" (high quality food served in a pub) experience, hit the two-level bar and restaurant known as **Lot No. 3** (460 106th Ave. Northeast, Bellevue, WA 98004; 425-440-0025; www.lotno3 .com; $$), where you will find mix-and-match sliders and snacks like Plate O' Bacon and artisan cheeses and meats. In Redmond, don't miss **Pomegranate Bistro** (18005 N.E. 68th St. Redmond, WA 98052; 425-556-5972; www.duparandcompany.com/pomegran ate-bistro; $$) for classic comfort food inspired by Chef Lisa Dupar's

Southern upbringing, classical French training, and passion for Northwest ingredients. Dine with the neighborhood regulars at **Bis on Main**, (10213 Main St., Bellevue, WA 98004; 425-455-2033, www .bisonmain.com; $$$) on Bellevue's Main Street, where you can always find fine dining, romance, and a fish of the day.

Destination Dining

For an enlightening dining experience, take the farm-to-table route with **Trellis** (220 Kirkland Ave., located in the Heathman Hotel, Kirkland, WA 98033; 425-284-5900; www.heathmankirkland.com/ html/trellis-restaurant.asp; $$$), where Executive Chef Brian Scheehser uses the finest produce harvested from his 10-acre farm in Woodinville along with other local ingredients to create the ultimate locavore meal. Sample his Two Hour Salad, with ingredients harvested within 2 hours of being served. Another memorable destination restaurant is **Cafe Juanita** (9702 N.E. 120th Place, Kirkland, WA 98034; 425-823-1505; www.cafejuanita .com; $$$$) where Chef Holly Smith pairs northern Italian cuisine with local, seasonal, and organic produce and a diverse selection of meats, fresh pasta, and creative vegetable dishes.

Head to the Willows Lodge in Woodinville to visit the **The Barking Frog** (14580 N.E. 145th St., Woodinville, WA 98072; 425-424-3900; www.willowslodge.com/wine_dine/barking_frog.html;

$$$), where Chef Bobby Moore showcases American regional cuisine with a Pacific Northwest influence in a warm bistro atmosphere.

For delicious Indian food, head to **Spice Route** (2241 148th Ave. Northeast, Bellevue, WA 98007; 425-643-4144; www.spice routecuisine.com; $$), for southern Indian food with northern Indian combinations, and Indochinese dishes that are packed with flavor and lots of spice. They also have a large variety of vegetarian and vegan dishes. Beat the rush at the lunch buffet by coming in at noon or get there before 7:30 in the evening, before the place fills up with Indian families that dine in the later hours.

Facing East Taiwanese Restaurant (1075 Bellevue Way Northeast, Suite B, Bellevue, WA 98004; Bellevue; 425-688-2986; $$) offers authentic Taiwanese fare. Wait times are long, especially on weekends. Don't miss the restaurant's many teas, sweet desserts, and beverages like shaved ice and milk teas. Recommended: the Taiwanese Pork Burger, a slice of braised pork belly sandwiched in a steamed bun with a tangy-sweet mixture of pickled mustard greens, crushed peanuts, sugar, and cilantro.

For Chinese Szechuan cuisine, go to downtown Bellevue's **Bamboo Garden** (202 106th Place N.E., Bellevue, WA 98004; 425-688-7991; www.bamboogardendining.com; $$), where people know to go for the Swimming Fire Fish. If Chinese menu items seem overwhelming and hard to decide then follow the thumbs-up symbol all throughout the menu which showcases the 30 most popular dishes. For the adventurous gastronome, look no further than the "Take a Walk on the Wild Side" part of the menu, which caters to those looking for extra spicy thrills or rarely found authentic dishes.

Downtown Bellevue's **Din Tai Fung** (700 Bellevue Way NE, Ste 280; Bellevue; WA 98004; 425-698-1095, www.dintaifungusa.com) is known for the highly popular *xiao long bao*—steamed juicy pork soup dumplings, hand-made daily in house. Don't miss any of the pork buns, wontons, rice cakes, or other tasty items on the menu. This is the first domestic franchise of this internationally recognized Taiwanese restaurant. The lines to grab a seat may be long but definitely worth the wait.

Sweets, Gifts & More

Some Seattle favorites also have shops on the Eastside such as **Cupcake Royale** (see p. 3), **Trophy Cupcakes** (see p. 13), **Top Pot Doughnuts** (see p. 53), **Fran's Chocolates** (see p. 6), and **Oh! Chocolate** (see p. 50).

Belle Pastry (10246-A Main St., Bellevue, WA 98004; 425-289-0015; second location in Seattle) is a casual French bakery with treats like fresh breads (including baguettes and brioche), apple or chocolate tartlets, croissants, napoleons, lemon cakes, and more. For Japanese pastries, look no further than **Fumie's Gold** (10045 N.E. 1st St., Suite CU2, Bellevue, WA 98004; 425-223-5893) with items like green tea mousse cakes and mini flourless muffins, cheesecakes, and fluffy strawberry shortcakes made with whipped cream icing. Another favorite Japanese bakery is **Fuji Bakery Inc.** (1502 145th Place Southeast, Bellevue, WA 98007; 425-641-4050;

www.fujibakeryinc.com; second location in Seattle), where you can find fresh breads and sandwiches. Try the curry bread, a deep-fried pastry filled with curry in spicy and mild versions; breads filled with red bean paste made of organic adzuki beans; or the popular cream puffs.

Kirkland has a selection of bakeries such as **Hoffman's Fine Cakes & Pastries** (226 Parkplace Center, Kirkland, WA 98033; 425-828-0926; www.hoffmansfinepastries.com), a European bakery with an assortment of cakes, like the popular princess torte made of sponge cake, raspberry jam, Bavarian whipped cream, and covered with marzipan; and coffee cakes; Danishes; croissants; strudels; and more. **The French Bakery** (219 Kirkland Ave., Kirkland, WA 98033; 425-898-4510) is where you can find fresh breads, croissant, tarts, and cakes. When strolling through Kirkland, don't miss the boutique bakery known as **Sweet Cakes** (128 Park Lane, Kirkland, WA 98033; 425-821-6565; www.sweetcakes kirkland.com) for cupcakes, dessert bars, cannoli, cheesecakes, and tarts. They also offer special-event cakes and gluten-free pastries. For truffles, creams, and other handcrafted chocolates, don't miss out on **Amore Chocolates & Gifts** (10149 Main St., Bellevue, WA 98004; 425-453-4553; www.amorechocolatesonmain.com). Last but not least, if you like food-related browsing, stop by **Oil & Vinegar** in the Bellevue Square Shopping Center (2086 Bellevue Sq., Bellevue, WA 98004; 425-454-8497; www.bellevuesquare.oilandvinegarusa .com) for a huge selection of vinegars and oils that work perfectly as gifts, or just have fun tasting your way through the store.

Appendix A:
Eateries by Cuisine

Bars, Pubs, Gastropubs & Lounges

Appendix B: Index of Purveyors

Index